DAVID AND JONATHAN

By the same author:

Zen and the Art of Post-modern Canada
The Dangers of Critical Thought

Cataloguing in publication data (Canada)

Schecter. Stephen, 1946-

David and Jonathan : a story of love and power in Ancient Israel

ISBN 1-895854-66-0

1. David, King of Israel - Poetry.   2. Jonathan (Biblical figure) - Poetry.   I. Title

PS8587.C433D38 1996   C811'.54   C96-940800-5
PS9587.C433D38 1996
PR9199.3S33D38 1996

Our ever-evolving catalogue is available
on the World Wide Web at our Internet site:

http://rdppub.com

Stephen Schecter

DAVID AND JONATHAN
A story of love and power in Ancient Israel

Robert Davies Publishing
MONTREAL-TORONTO-PARIS

Copyright © 1996, Stephen Schecter
ISBN 1-895854-66-0

Robert Davies Publishing,
311-4999 Saint-Catherine Street,
Westmount, Quebec, Canada H3Z 1T3

☎ 1-800-481-2440 / 1-514-481-2440

📰 1-888-RDAVIES

Distributed in Canada by General Distribution Services

☎ 1-800-387-0141 / 1-800-387-0172
📰 1-416-445-5967;

in the U.S.A., from General Distribution Services,
Suite 202, 85 River Rock Drive, Buffalo, NY 14287

☎ 1-800-805-1083

In the UK, by Drake International Marketing

For all other countries, please order from publisher.

e-mail: rdppub@vir.com

Visit our Internet website: http://rdppub.com

The publisher takes this opportunity
to thank the Canada Council and the
Ministère de la Culture du Québec (Sodec)
for their continuing support of publishing.

כָּל־אַהֲבָה שֶׁהִיא־תְלוּיָה בְדָבָר בָּטֵל דָּבָר, בְּטֵלָה אַהֲבָה; וְשֶׁאֵינָהּ תְּלוּיָה בְדָבָר, אֵינָהּ בְּטֵלָה לְעוֹלָם. אֵיזוֹ הִיא אַהֲבָה, שֶׁהִיא־תְלוּיָה בְדָבָר, זוֹ אַהֲבַת אַמְנוֹן וְתָמָר; וְשֶׁאֵינָהּ תְּלוּיָה בְדָבָר, זוֹ אַהֲבַת דָּוִד וִיהוֹנָתָן:

— פִּרְקֵי אָבוֹת, פרק חמישי, יט

All love that is conditional on something — when that something is gone, so is the love; but love that is conditional on nothing lasts forever. What love is that which is conditional on something? That is the love between Amnon and Tamar. And what love is conditional on nothing? That is the love between David and Jonathan.

— *Ethics of the Fathers,*
Chapter 5, Verse 19

Prologue

When Samuel, the last judge of Israel, was old, the people came and asked him to give them a king. Samuel chose Saul from the tribe of Benjamin. Soon after his election, Samuel came to Saul and ordered him to go to war against the Amalekites. He was to destroy them to the last child and take no booty, but Saul relented. He spared their king Agag and allowed the Israelites to take home the choice of the Amalekites' sheep and oxen. When Samuel heard of this, he went in person to kill Agag and told Saul that God, in anger at this betrayal of His commandment, would not allow his son to inherit his throne. Unbeknownst to Saul, Samuel then went to Bethlehem and anointed David, son of Yishai, the future king of Israel. After which Samuel retired to Ramah and no longer advised the king.

The Philistines, who were constantly at war with Israel, attacked Saul and his army in the hills of Judah. They were led by a great lord, Goliath, who challenged the Israelites to man-to-man combat. David, who came to visit his brothers in Saul's camp, took up Goliath's challenge and slew him with a stone from his slingshot. Saul took David into his household and kept him on at court, but Jonathan, Saul's son, fell in love with David and took him as his lover.

1

Imagine them, the two of them,
naked,
Jonathan hanging over the bed
a sheet across his loins
but David sitting on the floor
without a stitch.
He is red,
the other one is black.
'Gingy', they will say one day
as if he didn't belong.

Jonathan laughs.
David giggles like a girl.

Jonathan scratches his chest,
lets his hand play with his scrotum:
"So Saul has smitten in the thousands,
but David in the tens of thousands.
Aren't you a marvel?
And to think I sleep with you."
David says nothing.
"My father won't like it.
He likes to be on top,
well thought of,
head and shoulders above any man, said Samuel.
It went to his head. Never mind.
How about a kiss, my champion,
for the one man who loves you?"

Red David turns redder:
"Leave me alone."

But Jonathan won't leave him alone.
His eyes are dark and flashing
and the memory of a moment ago
licks at his underlips
like the flame that burns but does not consume.
"Leave you alone?" his lips twist like a bent spoon.
"Why don't you ask for the kingdom while you're at it?
Then you could simply banish me
like some unlucky concubine.
It's true. I'm like those women
singing beneath the window,
only their hero is in my bed
screwing me to the floor
the way he nailed Goliath to his own forehead.
The giant fell to a stone. I will not fall.
Not with both my legs around your neck.
Your sling will never have enough force."

David smiles, sadness stealing across his face
like a lizard over a rock.
"Maybe I won't have to banish you."

A man shifts in a bed.
An eyebrow arches as it does for centuries.
"What do you mean?"

"Your father will ask me to marry your sister."
Silence. Disbelief. A question in the eye of blindness.
"It is the way of kings.
When they can't kill you they bind you."

"But – "

"But I will not.
One, I do not love her.
Two, I have not earned her.
Three, my own father is still alive."

It was Jonathan's turn to grow quiet.
Light-heartedness drained from his heart
and the white face grew whiter,
pale with lover's fright beneath the black curls.
He looked at the man, the boy,
the slender reed like shepherd's grass
sitting in the centre of the room,
lion clubber, bear killer,
smart as a whip
and graced with the courage of God
telling him not to worry,
holding nothing against him,
not even his joking with love,
not even his playing with fire
against which little boys have been warned
from one generation to the next,
the worst fire love,
the worst joke treating it lightly,
taking it so much for granted
you can tell the one you love the most
he does not love you enough,
accuse him in advance of betrayal,
dare him to cast you off
at the very moment you are absolutely convinced
you have bound him forever,
have driven your soul like a stake
into his sly body.
And then the angels come,
little messengers of fate clothed in words
to show you what you fear most:
he does not love you enough.
Jonathan had counted again:
one,
two,
three.
He is still missing,
but the angels make him smile
the ill-at-ease smile of a bride.

David draws his fingers over the tiles,
purple borders around sheaves of barley
green, yellow, burnt orange radiant,
traces the awns
that fall across each corner for the poor:
he is a descendant of charity,
of light that struck a woman's hair
twice in the turning of the day,
and of lust.
So his fingers think
while his lover watches and blinks his eyes
to forget about the future,
about the pain gripping his heart like an oracle,
about time coming to an end
on some barren hillside.
Israel's first royal prince
rises from the bed like a spider,
alights on the fired clay
and jumps softly, a four by four human pod,
until his nude torso shadows
the shoulder of his father's retainer.
Sadness at noon.

*

Later. Still act one. Scene two.
Saul has offered and been refused once.
He has only one daughter left
to entice David into battle.
He plans his moves carefully,
wants love to strike
at an angle that will checkmate
the man he fears is God's minion.
Only fears.
Saul does not know
that Samuel had long ago gone to Bethlehem
with a calf and a horn of oil,
and as the fat of the heifer burned
anointed the eighth in the circle of brothers,
the red-haired one with beautiful eyes

mud deep with sorrow.
He only knows he has not seen Samuel or God
in donkey's years.
What he has seen day after day
is the torn edge of Samuel's coat
he had ripped with his own hand
when the judge turned to leave
and Saul's hand had cried for pity;
but instead of pity came prophecy:
"As you have torn my coat
so God will tear your kingdom."
Saul's memory is long,
as happens to people who cease to talk to God.
He remembers Samuel added:
"And give your kingdom to your friend
who is better than you."
And thinks:
"Better to the power of ten."
And thinks some more:
"I was too blunt last time.
Here, I said, take Merav my eldest,
only lead my troops in exchange.
And he said God forbid,
abased himself before the king,
pled father, brothers, flocks:
'I am a harp player, sire,
Goliath was an accident'."

Saul walked down cool halls in a lonely palace,
the white walls of fresh stone
and the mortar itself still wet like the king.
"Saul," cried the stones,
"remember when you first set out
from your father's house
in search of stray asses?
How little you thought you would wind up here,
first king of the first palace,
with no training but your good looks
and the might of your arm.
The seer called you a good man

and sent you on your way,
as if it were enough to be son to a warrior
in order to be king.
He who spent his childhood in the House of the Lord
learning the tricks of the trade
gave you no such chance,
plucked you walking down a road
and set you up in council
primus inter pares, a fall guy.
But what judge ever loved a king?
So now you're on your own
and it's lonely as the wind,
lonelier than lonely
with his curse whistling in your ear
but his counsel sworn to silence.
A voice calls Saul! Saul!
and it sounds like the echo
of your own bicameral heart.
That's life, Saul,
it comes with the royal turf
of booty and oxen and the soldiers' clamour
and an enemy king begging for mercy.
No prisoners is a divine command
of memory that exists forever,
outlasts even stones like us.
Yours are a king's orders,
words from the mouth of a man
whose father always counted: livestock, fields, grain,
the pluses and minuses of marriage.
Count, Saul, carefully;
you have one daughter left."

*

Now it came to pass
as the stones counselled the king
and the evening breeze blew its promise of death
over the Benjamite's fortified hill,
that Michal, sweet Michal,
the king's youngest and most beloved

and his last remaining,
dark like her brother but beneath the curls
a face lit with laughter,
alive and always running
after whatever did her in,
rope, sand, an orchard of pomegranates,
boys with their flashing smiles and strong legs,
thornstruck and ignorant:
love hurts, war bleeds,
life is very, very short;
that Michal, sweet Michal,
sat beneath the east wind
and blessed it with her scents
of myrrh and aloes
freed from tiny pots,
love genies hiding in darkness,
behind ears, dabbed beneath locks,
smoothed into the pitcher handle
between breast and arm
that still finds its way
onto jars and into rooms
where pen puts onto resined stock
words of calculated perfume
to snare a man.

Michal has seen her brother
dress David with his soul
and undress him with his eyes,
has seen David blush at table
on the inside of his own skin,
trapped between steak and stare
in a love of his own making
he no longer knows
is love or not love
betrothed to his intestines.
She has seen David rise and follow
though he is often the first to leave,
has less often caught his glance
to let him see laughter
glint iron through her branches of curls,

but enough, she knows, for it to lodge
like a metal plate in his brain
and disturb the embrace of red on black
when later her brother again
asserts his princely tyranny.
She has considered this matter for a while now
and has concluded it is hopeless
to hope for a miracle
other than death.
She has also concluded
that extreme measures will not be necessary.
Her brother was an accident
the man from Bethlehem had not foreseen
in his comings and goings:
harp music for a king,
sandwiches for his conscript brothers,
God's armour for the weak-chested tribes,
not thinking for a minute
that the still young flesh
he brought alone into battle
would cause the prince's eyes to bolt
and latch onto loneliness
more nude than any exposed limbs
in the valley of the Philistine's taunts.
The man from Bethlehem
had herded his loneliness so long
he wore it like an undergarment,
had watched and waited as time passed
and let time pass,
watched and waited as desire fell into time
and let it fall,
let the fever pass as his nipples yearned
for the brush of lips
and his sex strained against the heat
of the skillet-hanging sun
and his mind saw time
traipse like a woman
on a hilltop he could not reach;
had first cried out and then some
until his cries fell into the valley

and his mouth fell upon the cries,
and he out of this silence
smithlike fashioned valour,
and out of valour faith,
and out of faith forgetfulness,
until one day he showed up at court
and cleaved Jonathan's soul
with innocence the glimmer of brass
declined from the king.
Michal laughed to herself:
Jonathan was not supposed to happen
but Jonathan did
and he was caught,
waylaid,
heart surprised,
and groped now like a blind man
for the mantle of the king.
She liked that,
liked to see him in disarray
and half in love with her brother,
a looking glass to her own sense
of no misgivings.

And so she sat before twilight
throwing the dice of love:
Saul wanted David close,
obligated,
fealty sworn to his son's inheritance,
not loosely bound by night sheets.
He knew his son was noble,
courageous,
and weak;
and knew the mix was lethal for the crown.
Michal also wanted David close.
She liked the way he moved,
went to battle in straps,
looked away from her brother
while his body stayed loyal,
and more than body;
soul.

That was a plus. Her brother could be murdered
in his bed.
Not she.
She wanted him for something else,
for all the boys she dusted off
amid the olive trees.
She wanted him
because he would always slip away,
a man like a house divided.
But unlike her sister
she wanted him,
and that was her trump card.

When her father came in
a single-braceleted arm
touched him at the elbow,
night breeze as woman,
daughter,
liege daughter to a king:
"Sire, my brother is everything,
handsome and strong
and fleet and brave
as you have made him.
But he is handsome without stealth,
strong without purpose,
fleet without aim,
brave without craft.
He is goodness itself
and will be undone
by his own goodness.
To save you once
he risked his life,
walked into the enemy camp
with no armour but his sword and boy
and so struck fear into the wretches
who mocked our own.
When our army of untrained farmers saw
what one foolhardy man could do
they gained a little courage,
came out from their caves

and added as best they could
to the Philistines' confusion,
descended with home-made axes, swords,
war-cries from the choked-up throats
of sinners avenging God
on a retreat become a rout.
You sought, Sire, to sculpt their paltry victory
into a national epic.
You enjoined them to refrain
from bringing lips to food until evening,
as if chase and slaughter
were made sublime by denial,
hoping between sunrise and sundown
to give tillers of soil
a shot of military discipline.
They all obeyed but one,
your son who was out of earshot
and ate with his boy in the wood,
their rods dipped in the honeycomb.
At the day's end tally
you discovered the losses were less than the shouts
and realized the Philistines had fled
more than fallen.
A victory of such proportions does not last.
The vanquished return. You debated
a policy of hot pursuit,
but no one stepped forward
to defend the yes position,
not even the Lord's priest.
The kingdom was still a patchwork
of fields and vineyards,
and your heart sank
and your wrath rose
and settled on my luckless brother,
who took the rap
for other people's cowardice, maybe fright.
He ate, you said,
and like a fool he said that it was good.
The people defended him: he did not know,
had not sworn, broke no oath.

Besides, had he not gone with his boy,
they would still be cowering in their caves.
You wept at such third-rate majesty.
King, you were ready to give them your son,
but they shrunk from crime
in a way they never shrunk from sin.
And so, like the Philistines,
you went home
until they returned
with the heavyweight champion of the world.
Even Jonathan trembled a bit.
But God is still with you
and sent you Yishai's boy,
a mixed blessing if ever there was, Father,
and yet a blessing:
one lopped head but tambourines in the streets,
a thousand hearts swooned
but only one conquered;
not your choice perhaps,
but again no oath is broken,
and David stays in your home,
house, hold.
I know his glory worries you,
the way it dazzles Jonathan
worries you more;
but I already told you:
my brother is good
and his goodness will undo him.
I am not dazzled, Father.
Give me the shepherd warrior
and bind him to our house."

But at once Saul thought
he could bind him to death,
and so assented.

Now: how to approach him?
How to overcome the shame
of a youth too poor to own armour
and a heart already sewn

to the flat-chested sex,
needle drawn through blood-swollen bone
to the skin of a prince?
How to cap his own heart's rage
and make it seem true
to this man who has already heard
the whistle of the king's spear
thudding into the wall like a question mark?
He set no store on love,
which he knew the young would handle
with their usual cruelty.
He was more worried by the basics:
the shepherd boy's pride
whittled by hand-me-down tasks –
'David, carry the slops to the field, pen up the sheep,
take blankets and love to your brothers
but hurry home, you're all I have,
fingers disgracing a harp' –
and the pride stripped of its leaves like an artichoke
until the man has become
as light as his music but not simple,
and so deceives all but the king
who knows the lad will come to grief,
broken as they all will break
on his own lightness.
Saul therefore steps warily,
cups David's lightness as if it were his own
and for a moment turns it to good account:
"Play," he asks as much as a king can ask,
and shuts his eyes
hoping to shut the rage,
listens to the long silent sound of God
this jack-of-all-trades plucks from the harp
that turns his lips to repose,
spear to hushed scarlet smile.
For a moment they are at peace,
grief to unknown grief.
Later Saul lets it be known
his second daughter loves David
with his approval,

encourages rumour to pass
down the chain of his household
that the voice of bride and groom
will soon be raised to the hills of Judah
until what was once a mining prospectus
has become a sure-fire investment
with no way out.
The king has even forsworn a dowry
so great is the delight he seeks to cast
from steward to slave over this enterprise.

*

"All he asked for was a hundred Philistine foreskins,"
David finally rasped to Jonathan
that morning he was pinned to the bed
like a chief accountant called in on the carpet
because the figures did not add up.

"And you gave him double the number,"
Jonathan shot back,
"eager to prove how little beholden you are –
'If it's all the same with you, King,'
I'd rather you take two hundred samples
of enemy manhood,
a c-note for your daughter,
another century for me' –
as if you were a walking IOU:
'Remember. When it comes to Philistines I'm your man'.
Signed David, son-in-arms."
And Jonathan kept his lover
as pinioned as his tears
while he tried to teach him, tell him,
pump sperm into him where words were useless
because what he had to say
had nothing to do with words,
they were too slow, too crafted,
laid over with time to cover one's rear
and make everything seem less dangerous,
but Jonathan cried through his sweat to David

that he was beholden, more than he thought,
and even more to the king
who would call him to arms
and chew at his victories
like indigestible licorice
until murder was the only solution,
and if not murder flight,
which to Jonathan came up the same wrong number;
and all this his semen
slipped into David's bowels
before words again went to war:
"Of all the women, why her?
Why a woman? Why anyone?" –
each question pettier than the first
and complicated by blood,
though brain-in-the-groin, like brain-in-the-stars,
knows they are one and the same,
the one every lover has asked
knowing it neither needs
nor merits an answer
because there never is one
more reasonable than the question.
And yet Jonathan asked the question.
And David had no answer.

See, then:
hurt sizzling in the heart
like sirloin strips on a grill.
Finally hurt or heart cools down;
leaves the two warriors
twined in their chequer-board embrace.
They cannot help the words,
the deeds,
the long arm of history.
They love each other far too much.
Jonathan pulls back to look
at the red head of hair, red pubes,
red smile on this ordinary bundle
of gristle and veins
shaped for reasons that escape even God

when He's looking for a new beloved
into his sour candy of happiness.
There flesh is puffed at the elbow,
cheek stubble grows like barley seed,
legs whose soft hairs beg his fingers
stretch below his own;
the whole picture is one of promise
not even betrayal can erase.
When Jonathan looks he sees his lover's touch,
sees his hand, lips, back of arm, thigh,
any bit of limb that brushes his skin
with miracle.
To that there is no resistance
and he offers none,
plunges instead into his lover's body
that folds and folds and folds
like giftwrapping.
David also sees more than he says,
even when all he sees is the ceiling
as Jonathan talks to his chest:
"You knew, didn't you,
from the first moment I saw you
my soul flew to your flesh
like a bandaid to a wound.
It is not a pretty image but that
is how it is.
I stuck to you
like a dried tear,
like the hot east wind,
like spikenard essence,
here
and here
and here,"
and he touches his lover's neck,
armpit,
groin.
"No, I am not woman,
not crazed,
still have words to show you
I can think like any man,

and when the words falter admit:
what I feel belongs to the ineffable,
to the nameless,
to the fallen petals and the evaporated dew
and the severed head and the lopped foreskin,
even, if you will, to love fried in its own hurt.
But when you leave me
what I do not have cries in pain
as sharp as any that would scream
were you to slit my side."
Jonathan plays with the sunbleached hairs
around his lover's nipples,
his fingers rope and smooth
these last blond remnants of fur
as if they were wheels
spinning and undoing:
hemp, flax, the gold of forgetfulness.
His index circles the brown nut
until it is erect
and he surprised when amnesic fingers
feel its spear tip beneath their touch.
He has done this so many times
he knows it by heart,
the way the hairs lie down like grass,
the flesh yields, the earth breathes,
a man's nipple cuts
love that has slipped into habit.
He has been playing for time,
for breath, for the wind of prophecy
to alight upon him
and open his voice to what he knows.
He wants to tell his lover
what has already come to pass,
tell himself,
tell and console:
"You have married my sister
because she is daughter
to the king whose son you love.
You think this will make things right;
my father will lay off,

my sister settle for half the house,
you will be free to come and go
and kill Philistines as you please.
You think even you will believe
you want a woman but not a crown.
This is not very good thinking,
and for once my father will agree with me.
He will send you to war and watch you return
more a hero than ever,
and the praise from young girls' lips
will kindle his votive rage
as the priest's fire the bullock.
He will watch you enter my room and think
nothing has changed yet all is worse:
now he, meaning you, has sister and brother.
His thinking too is not very good,
but it is understandable, and he is king.
I do not know what my sister thinks.
I hear her call inside you
like an amputated limb
and almost go crazy from the silence.
She has what I do not
and that draws you to her.
This too is understandable but I do not understand:
your nipple is too erect for my mind,
my hand too much at home
as it skims over your breast,
dark caress on a velvet gourd
so fine there need be no other.
I should not talk like this to you.
It makes you flinch, your head run,
your heart burn for sin
extraordinary."
And so Jonathan grew still.
David beside him says nothing.
What can he say to this man
with spies in his own mind?
That it is God's design, perhaps?
Perhaps, but David is clever enough
to hold that answer in reserve.

His sins will increase, as his lover has said.

*

And it came to pass
as Jonathan had foretold.
Saul sent David on more expeditions
from which he returned triumphant.
His name grew ever dear, Saul's rage kept pace.
Michal's love for David waxed and let the king stew.
It was checkmate at every turn.
God's design, you might say,
but Saul had forgotten God,
had even stopped buying carpets.
Slowly the king stepped over the line,
unburdened himself to his son:
"Your sister is enamoured with the Yishai boy,"
Saul dropped like poison into Jonathan's ear.
"I find it excessive, unseemly,
as if she were vying
with all the maidens of Israel
for her own husband's affection.
A man has no right to turn the head
of his own wife, least of all a man
who has already turned another's."

Jonathan listened like a tree.

"When she came to me to sue
for her own hand in marriage,
she spoke to me of you:
so good, she said, he'll be played for a sucker.
You were a blind, I was the sucker
It seems wherever that harp player smiles
hearts crack as well as minds,
people forget their sense of place,
men take out their handkerchiefs
and women toy with the kingdom
as though it were a doll's house.
They have quickly forgotten

how at Ramah they beleaguered Samuel
for a king. Enemies, they cried,
besiege us on all sides,
and we wait like dumb dispersed sheep
asking to be fleeced.
Thus Samuel found me looking for strays.
King material, he said, and sent me to prophesy.
And the people wondered: is Saul among the prophets?
But of all men I was least made
to follow a rope of dung interpreters.
I will turn the country into a corral,
was my promise; predators beware.
Most are gone. Only the Philistines
lurk about the premises, and even they,
my enemies unto death, are wary.
Israel has a crown. At night its head thinks,
studies reports, plots campaigns
in which the stripling son-in-law
reaps honour, praise, love,
while the people murmur still:
is Saul among the prophets?
No, Saul is at home
watching his house decompose."

Still like a tree Jonathan says nothing,
waits for his father's final word
to cut his own lips like a razor.

"I would be rid of that man,"
the blood red sentence at last spills forth.

Only then does Jonathan speak.
First to himself:
"And I? Do you think I do not hurt,
my sleep so unlike yours
each time I turn over
to find he has gone to my sister?
But better an empty bed for an evening
than a lifetime of cold sheets –
and who am I to tell him what to do?"

Then aloud:
"It looks bad, but are looks all?
My sister has her reasons, so does he,
and what harm they do, if harm it is,
shall strike first at their door. And yet I wish it not,
for nothing will sate revenge but all our bloods.
And if you can't remember that, remember this:
what wrong has David ever done you
but kill Goliath and drop two hundred foreskins
at the footstool of your throne?
The people praise him for it, and that rankles you.
But think: what more could you want?
A lieutenant finally does his job,
gives confidence to the people
they have chosen their king wisely.
Or does Saul need his name dragged through the sky
for history to record
what women hanging out the wash have begrudged him?
Slander is a pittance next to murder, Father."
On that he shuts up, thinking he has said
one word too many. Perhaps he has.
The scale of blood is a delicate thing
and many bloods hang here in the balance.

Picture them; father and son in this field
which one day will be a valley of death.
Shoulder to shoulder they stand
lipsealed and bent to the yellow fire
waiting for the future to pronounce itself.
The grass grows in clumps. Burrs stick to their knees.
It is very hot. Too hot for murder, thinks Saul,
and swears to his son
that as God lives so does David.

*

Reprieve is in the air.
It has its own excitement,
like hot summer nights
that run a fever through the heart.

Jonathan runs to David
to tell him all that has happened,
tells him as one who believes his words
and the words already an embrace:
"Come, my love, all will be as yesterday,
and as the day before yesterday."
But the day before yesterday
David was married,
and yesterday Jonathan had warned
no good would come of that.

Those who love forget,
a historian thousands of years hence
would remind their people.

David did not forget. He looked,
looked and looked at this man erect before his eyes
with eyes like baskets of golden apples
and lips that sent him prayers
to caress the flesh above his shoulder blades,
the verses slipping like felt arrows
through the thin family clothes.
He looked even as he gathered him up
and drew him to his arms
and from his arms to the bed
where all prayers are eventually buried.
"You are my friend," he said.
"You are my lover and my wife's brother.
Three is always the limit.
I come from border country.
The hills look down their noses
to the dropped valley below,
its flat table runneled with varicose veins
parched where they should be blue.
When the sun slips behind the last ridge
the blue finally comes out,
but the blue belongs to the hillside,
to the packed earth and stone
that lean into the mountain for the night
like tucked away silver.

Down below it is another story.
Dusk is in no hurry.
Every day the slaked ground swells
to the iron laced hue of gold.
Before the hills look down there lies the town.
Long robes, brown shutters, donkeys, spices;
it is the one place that never changes colour.
I hate it. It is mean and miserable
and black with the garb of venerable men
picking their noses with their wisdom.
Your sister knew that right away
and she'd never been to Bethlehem.
She knows the way she laughs. Her breasts swell
like the land back of the Jordan;
just like yours.
You do not think that is right.
Even your breathing
disapproves of my telling you this.
Yet what am I to do
lying here next to you
while so much of life disapproves of itself?
When the prophet came to fetch me
I was tending my sheep,
seated on a rock and lording over desert
with my knife at work on bread and cheese
and thinking about the knife;
the way it cuts, pares,
glints in the despotic sunlight,
while below the land heaves and cracks with lust.
I could have stayed a long time, all my days perhaps,
built myself a shelter and sat back
to sink my mind into old gold.
But what brought the prophet brought the king's men,
and I left; came to court to sing for your father
and fell into your arms
Gold from head to foot if ever I saw it,
and more trouble than Bethlehem.
Your sister saw me in your arms
and decided it should be otherwise,
and now your father's cup runneth over.

You think your father will relent
because for a moment God changed his mind
and helped him surmount his own heart.
I think it might have been best
had my mind stayed suncaked as nuggets at twilight.
But we have slept together and will,
though your sister has her claims
and the king has tasted murder."

Jonathan was almost seduced.
He heard love and heard his love leaving him
in one and the same confidence.
A war started up in his breast:
armies, dust, afterwards a shrub in the sand,
beside it a corpse still as heat.
He turned to the man lying next to him
and promised they'd be careful;
and then they laughed like two serpents in a bell jar,
smooth, freckled, taking great care.

Michal was just as careful.
True to her word
she watched David come and go,
listened to the maidens gossip and praise
and to her brother struggle with his happiness.
Her skirts were spread wide with laughter;
it was her antidote to springtime.
And so it happened, as happens now and then,
that the lovers behaved wisely.

*

The war changes theatres.
News comes to Saul:
again the Philistines are arming.
It is not bad news, he thinks,
a battle brings matters to a head;
and while he is quite prepared to wait
for the domestic issue to break out in boils,
he find the days long and the wait trying.

The old find it hard
when the young seem to have wound their way
back into paradise.
It is then that used lips smack together:
the smell of burned villages
will soon have them get their clothes on.
Saul knows he is taking a chance.
War has not helped him before,
but what is merely trying can turn
into the insufferable.

David is sent out; strikes, and strikes again
until the hobbled Philistines conclude
it is time to crawl home and lament their gods.
When David returns
the streets are no noisier
than any day save the Sabbath,
but in every eye congratulations,
in every greeting love.
David lays down his sword and takes up his harp
at the footstool of the king.
To Saul
nothing is worse than this simple music.
Of all things he least expected
things would pick up where they left off
and he lose his mind
in the bosom of his family.
The harpsound drives him crazy.
As though a woman with long fingernails
sleeks music through his hair designed to soothe
but does not soothe.
Cannot.
Like a river, a harpsound brings peace
to those who are at peace,
and Saul is not at peace.
He is on edge,
and on the edge of this edge reclines his heart
like a liver in another religion,
the notes pecking away like birds.
He cannot understand how one man

can have so much luck
and of all men this one,
young, fair-haired, guileful,
and no one able to see past innocence,
they are all drunk on love – on luck –
only Saul able to perceive
history has condemned the king
in his own lifetime.
Even his children tell him to calm down
lest his rage become handmaiden
to his own destiny,
but the very thought of being anyone's maid
drives his rage past the boiling point of jam,
and the fingers which have taken over his mind
turn the javelin on its centre of gravity
as they stare eyeless as dumb knuckles
at a bull's-eye called murder in the second degree.
When Saul finally wakes from his anger
the spear is stuck in the wall opposite.
He weeps to find it so lonely.

*

David has fled to his wife's chambers.
On his face death still hangs like gauze.
Michal knows at once
that what she has for months been expecting
has come to pass.
And deals with it, expeditiously.
"If you don't leave now, you wake up a dead man."

His mouth agape turns to a block of wood.

She answers the stopped words
with the widow's smile she has long prepared:
"I shall miss you, of course,
your red crown that falls to the pillow
and your lips that yield to lips announcing betrayal,
the evenings we have laughed and schemed
to keep us all happy,

though we both knew it could not last.
Saul is a good man
but his mind goes hunting in his body,
and his body, like his heart, farmer tall and true
and bewildered by his children and God.
We can neither kill him nor depose him;
prudence therefore dictates we forgive him
though he takes so much away" –
and she opened her robe for him to see,
and brought his hand to touch her shining breasts
and weeping sex and full-length cry raw upon her skin:
"There. Your fingers now have something to remember;
but for now they'd best be used
to let yourself out my bedroom window."

Already they could hear sentries posted at the door.
Michal went to the cupboard
and drew forth the spare set of sheets
husband and wife knotted together
and tied to the bed, then tossed into the night.
David had one leg over the sill
when Michal brought her lips to his
and bade him take care with her brother.
Then he was gone,
the white ladder pulled up,
folded,
returned to its drawer,
as the whispers started to make their rounds
about what a bad deal she got;
but Michal knew it is sometimes a blessing
to disappear from history,
so when David slipped down the bedsheets
she also made her exit.

Michal took the teraphim and put them in the bed,
bunched goatskins up for a pillow,
then got in next to her husband
to wait for morning to rap at the door:
"The king wants to see his son-in-law,"
was the way the officer broke the peace.

Timidly Michal answered her husband was sick,
as they could see for themselves;
and so it was reported to the king
by his empty-handed messengers.

But Saul was neither Isaac nor Laban.
His memory was longer
and he knew how to consult it:
idols and goat hair
were part of a woman's bag of tricks
to throw a father off the scent.
"Fools," he cried, "go and fetch him bed and all."

Of course, when they got there the bed was empty.
The sergeant-at-arms' face paled sharp,
his bowels dropped in terror,
all he had for the king
was this tithe of a bolster.
When the king saw this show and tell
he let out a laugh like dry ice
and his fury stayed like that,
short, bitter, reined in by its kin;
his anger mocked his anger,
his shame mocked his shame,
even his terrible sadness
took on the air of a well known cheat.
He did, however, allow himself
a few words with his daughter:
"Why like this? Why deceive me?
When you wanted him, words spilled from your tongue
like ants after honey; when I want him,
you turn mute and do as you please,
forget that besides being your father
I am king.
It was my enemy you sent on his way."
And now his mouth full of ants adds:
"Yours too,
all of ours."

But Michal had resigned

and the king seemed to have understood.

"He made me do it," she lamely offered.
"'Why make me kill you?' he said."
That was all she told before starting
her descent to a common life,
keeping to herself what she had learned:
such a man is no enemy,
a father cannot protect a son,
sometimes the limelight will kill a king;
and thought with pleasure of the man's long staff
pointed on her sofa to the sun,
smiling at this strange parting between body and soul
like land that has severed the Dead Sea
from the Mediterranean.

*

David fled to Ramah, to Samuel,
to the one man with a cloak
large enough to protect him.
He arrived out of breath,
the shadows of night still pinned to his shoulders
and hungry as a boy is hungry,
first for bread,
then for a chance to tell his story.
Samuel listened to it all,
to what was said and left unsaid,
and sighed for all concerned
though no sound left his lips.
He then took David by the arm
and led him into the garden:
"God told me Saul, I crowned him king,
knowing he and the fools who asked for him
were a mistake. Saul tried,
but he's as weak as he is tall,
and I had to look for a successor.
No one knows that's you save your sheep,
the fish in my pool, and this olive tree
that daily has to listen to an ex-judge

second guess his own judgment
and bide the useless years that drag at his shoulders
like a second, heavy cloak out of season."
And Samuel lifted up his arm,
that great thunderous arm of his
whose sleeve hangs down like the Lord's cowl
and even now makes grown men bolt
their little paths of consolation.
"It seems we're having visitors."
David squinted into the distance
and saw brass glint on men's chests.
"Do not worry. The king sends armed messengers
to a village without walls. He is more foolish
than I thought."

When the king's messengers approached the town,
prophets went to greet them with prayer and food.

"The king wants his son-in-law."

"It ill befits a king to want
and least of all a boy."

"Then the king commands."

"The king above that king forbids."

And so it went, chapter and verse, well into the evening.
By daylight they were gone as they had come.
Back at the palace a disappointed king
listens to a garbled report:
"Samuel....prophets....pardon, Sire..
it seemed to make sense at the time."
Because Saul can remember a time
when it also made sense to him,
he thanks them for their failure.
After they are dismissed he calls for replacements.
"Listen," he tells them, "David has run
to hide behind Samuel's skirts.
I want him back.

That's simple enough, isn't it?
Only men of the Lord
stand between you and him,
and they are armed only with words.
Still, be careful; these words turn heads.
My last emissaries returned
with prophecies instead of a prisoner."

But Saul's words were not enough
to stem the flow from God's orifice.
"They came at us like a flock of wise geese.
Welcome! welcome! they cried,
and taking each man by the arm
pelted us with questions;
the questions led to drink and the drink to questions
until the boy as they called him
seemed a trifle indeed
before the double-breasted hills in the distance.
Excuse us, Sire, you had warned us,
but these men spin magic out of nothing,
out of air and sunlight, out of pebble and sky,
out of fruit heaped up on tables
laid end to end in the shade of olive trees,
and the trees old as tired dust
you'd have sworn they had heard Sarah laughing."
Thus did the second delegation report
what would befall the third
until Saul was forced to conclude
a king's errand required the king,
and took his pack of bones
to their second coronation.

There was no advance party
when Saul arrived at the village.
Noon.
Shut doors.
Stone still cats.
Ground dry as flat bread.
Saul stopped at the well.
Drank.

The tin cup clattered as it fell.
A leg twitched nearby.
The king asked directions of a stoop.
"David? Samuel?"
An arm pointed to the right,
and its fingers waved uphill.
Saul turned,
turned his beast.

Samuel was waiting in his doorway.

"He is old," thought Saul, "my God, how he is old.
And crazy as ever. The hair still in coils, hissing.
If only they would, he probably wishes."

"And you," thinks Samuel, always good at divining,
"a king's bearing but not a king,
and a crown worn like a duncecap."

But to start with they are polite;
each in his way is a man of God.
Saul is led out back, his feet are washed,
food and drink are placed before him.
Samuel does not partake;
prerogative of age, he explains.
Saul's lips stretch into a line of mercy.
"The boy," he begins.

"I know," says the old man, meaning you can't have him.

"No you don't! You have no idea.
He sneaks about with weasel eyes,
his hands pluck kindness and his tongue love,
his charm so great even you excuse
the way he stole into my house and title
and well before his time.
You see, I haven't forgotten
the torn coat and the torn kingdom.
You always had a gift for the vivid phrase,
but sometimes I wondered

if the voice that spoke through you were not your own,
the voice of a father
broken, angry, reviling his sons
for lining their pockets on the bench,
and I the breast-plate of your revenge.
My son is not like yours. He'd give up his life
for the next man, for the whole country if need be;
for what you believe in, honour above all.
He is ten times more a king than I ·
and yet he is only a prince
I fear will die a prince.
Because of you. Because of that man."
On that Saul's lips closed hard and tight
as lips foreclose on an oath.

Samuel takes the measure of those drawn lips
and replies:
"So you think I take the name of God in vain.
Silly man! You still haven't learned
there are some things in life
it is dangerous to disobey.
As if the world were a well of infinite pardon.
Let me tell you something, Saul.
I don't work any more. Judge, father, man of God –
I'm pensioned off. That's why you're king.
But if you want my advice, leave well enough alone.
Your son is still alive,
still respects you,
still commands respect.
The boy, as you call him, wishes him no ill,
rather the opposite from what I hear;
and one cannot love the son without the father.
As for God, like all of us,
you'd do well to shut your mouth
and open your ears."

The argument went on and on.
The olive tree grew black as the king's soul.
He didn't notice; forever young, valiant,
worried about the future.

Samuel let him rant.
Saul tore at his hair, rent his clothes,
left no stone unturned:
"Your work is done, you say,
forgetting I too am your work,
I, king, four cubits high crown,
who took this swell of plaintiffs off your hands
and lashed them tribe to tribe, head to head,
a bundle of sticks into a nation.
That's my throne, my house, my handiwork;
it should not be my shame,
a flimsy loincloth snatched by the least upstart
who can sweet-talk God with a song.
Doubtless we are all men when laid end to end,
but we arise into the world, put on garb, walk erect,
make plans as best we can
once we have come when called.
What more do you want?
It is not up to you to deny the king
you have set over the people,
a donkey's man who only asked after his donkeys.
I want the boy you shelter
from father and king."

A pin-hole of light in the distance,
but here it is already thick with night,
so thick you can almost touch the air
and a mouth closes on blackness
as if it were cotton. Out of such dark
a thick voice speaks for the defence:
"Take him. You are, as you say, the king.
But you have not come for that.
You have come for my assent,
the benediction of a retired judge
on your crazy plans for murder.
An elder statesman has only the power to refuse,
and I refuse. What's more, the people will know
you have taken the young man
without my approval and against my counsel.
We'll see then if your bundle of sticks

doesn't fly apart."

The answer strikes like a knife.
A great cry goes up from this man
naked by his own hand,
not a stitch of clothing left
to hide his rage and sorrow
because this old man is always right
to leave him in the lurch.
Naked, he wails to the night for justice,
his yellow crown askew,
his body trembling like shattered war plans.
Pity the king.
His fingers clutch rags
and his eyes weep onto his fingers.
His mouth bends close to the ground.
He'd eat the paltry grass if he thought it would help,
but God has forbidden the earth
to serve as of old as a court of appeal,
forcing Saul to address his complaints to the sky;
and so the royal sound of anguish
climbs the night to Heaven and screams
as you are my witness
to rocks piled high in a garden.
In the morning
Samuel's neighbours watch the beggar king
take his justice on the road out of town.
He is clad and alone,
but the rumours have already passed from house to house
and soon will leap from village to village
until the whole country will again be asking:
is Saul also among the prophets?

*

Now comes the worst part,
and the play is not half over.
At first you are relieved
to have escaped with your life.
You think of everything that lies ahead,

forgetting that a man or woman
has to look back in order to say
how very good it is.
So with David; a young man
under house arrest
in the home of a man
who has seen it all.
He eats three meals a day:
figs, dates, olives, cheese,
thyme-roasted lamb,
what ought to dress the old age table
of a prophet who has tried to avoid
seeing into the future.
With each meal comes a lesson:
clan maps, battle lists, songs of drowning horses,
the fine hard art of compromise
between the urges of man and God
that passes for government.
Each evening Samuel prays to God
to bridle his heir apparent
one more day,
for the days that grew short have now grown long,
and Samuel can hear
the eager momentum in the blood.
It is the time of kings.
Eyes drawn to court as they are to jewels;
the flesh would climb higher than the soul.
David feels the leash soft as love.
The old man is worried for the boy.
and fears civil war.
Not that he is afraid:
he knows the earth can soak up blood
with a greed it never knows when eating seed,
knows too on whose head he poured
oil from the horn;
but so many defeats has he had to swallow
thorn and thistle where there should have been grapes,
he would like to turn them to good account,
pawn them for patience
on behalf of this not-yet-ripe man

and the sundry third parties
he will wound by moving too fast.
David senses the old man's care
staked out like tent pegs to picket his soul,
and wonders how it is
he has once again drawn someone's heart
to struggle with his own.
The old man's counsel he knows is wise,
but it vies with the hurt and desire
that also whisper advice:
a king, his son,
a naked wife in the window,
one breast showing in the dim light
to prompt his mind to longing;
yes, he muses, those proud tits,
soft offering, and hiding a granite mind
that laughed with him at the simple level
of intrigue they undid in bed,
misses the intrigue,
misses the garland shouts of after battle
rising to his ears,
and when he doesn't miss he longs
for the brother with whom he cried
because his soul was seared when they coupled.
Against such odds
the love of an old man wrapped in caution
has not got a chance.
Still, it is not without its strengths,
for David feels forced to flee;
and there where the night is split in two
slips out of the house,
leaves only a curt note on the table
to wish his host the peace he takes away.
The long explanation he keeps to himself
for the dark hours between Naiot and the court
as he uses the stars to follow his wife's injunction:
take care of my brother, he repeats to himself,
unaware that sometimes you can change a life
by changing a preposition.
When Samuel rises to a morning roe

that looks in on the table,
he finds the few and carefully chosen words.
Biting his lips,
Israel's last seer turns his eyes south.

*

And so to the south.
Two days later.
Jonathan lies asleep
in the crack between night and day.
Roe eyes stare but belong to a man
who is wet with dew and shivers.
He shivers because he does not know
if the man asleep will rejoice to see him,
will take him in his arms
as he now wants to be taken,
having seen, again having seen
the black curls and the powerful arms
and the legs that open and close like scissors,
and that face that bares its neck
as much to a knife as to God.

David pulls himself up to the edge
and does a little reckoning:
once,
twice,
how many times can you leave a man
and return?
But when Jonathan opens his eyes,
he blesses David as he blesses his soul
for returning to his body.
And now for once, just for once,
black and red blend
in this castle parquetry,
the lust and fear that run to the colour of loathing
for once left outside like dead quail,
only the sleek and dripping limbs
of a man who has worn the woods like a nightshirt
allowed into the chamber,

the bed,
the still open aorta of love.
And for once, just for once, they are happy.

Hours later they wake up.
The sun high in the sky melts anything in sight.
In the space hollowed out of the wall
Jonathan sits
and looks into the garden.
His friend stands near, a fox on his hind legs.
They watch the earth at work, though nothing moves.
Fronds smile crazily. The trees keep guard
like a one man army. Shrubs that flower
disrobe.
Jonathan reaches for David's hand
and places it on his shoulder,
there where it flows into his neck;
in lieu of the words
he does not have to say
points to the grasses pushing their way
through the fire-baked earth
and into the fire-baked air,
bent by genes to the eyes of men
and a halogen sky,
and starts to name them:
calamus, cinnamon, thyme,
and the man whose fingers knead the word-soaked flesh
talks to him of the whereabouts
of love's other fruit trees:
the almond and the pomegranate,
frankincense and myrrh;
and so they sit and stand
in the shadows of stone
wedded to the murmurs of their bowels,
lords bestowing praise
as if theirs was the kingdom.
It was not.

Saul was soon informed of David's return,
but when Jonathan next sat down

at the king's table,
nothing was said;
not the next day either
nor the day after that,
until finally the son rose against the father
and overturned his cup
so the wine could flow like blood
and asked the man who sired him
to what purpose silence:
"It's too bad, isn't it, Father,
you can't slice me in two,
discard the Jonathan that is not your Jonathan
and keep the better half,
like the choice parts from the butcher shop.
Only it doesn't work that way.
From two one, but the one is indivisible:
a hand-me-down truth of humanity.
And another one that you taught me:
honour thy guest;
so even if, for argument's sake, he is only mine,
how long do you think I will feed him scraps
like a dog in the kitchen?
You want our love confined to quarters - you have it.
But that's as far as it goes.
I can no more give him up
than leave you to yourself.
Whole cloth, Father, one seamless bolt;
there will be time enough for rending."

Once again
Jonathan cut his anger short
and converted it to love.
Prince among men.
But Saul was a tower of rage,
head and shoulders smouldering
like a fire it is forbidden to extinguish.
And yet the king says nothing.
His eyes stare at half his son,
at the red-stained cloth,
at the visions that limn the future.

He thinks Jonathan a fool
who will do anything for a piece of ass,
but not that much a fool:
he has touched him to the quick
with his stories of father and son
ascending all the way to God.
It is true, thinks Saul, he does not approve
that a man should love another man –
his own father taught him that –
and he will neither condone nor abet
his son being turned into a wife.
And so, although he loves his son,
he cannot invite his friend to his table
without betraying himself,
his father,
his father's father,
even the woman he lay down with
in order to father this father in turn.
And then there is his twice-deserted daughter,
and that delicate question of the crown.
Damn fool! when you think about it.
He was happy with the current arrangements:
David banished to Ramah by common consent,
Saul's brow free to enjoy
the kingship and its dreams;
but now that the boy is back
Samuel's prophecies also stir.
Soon the winds will raid his sleep.
His mind, unmoored, will night fish in his heart.
And in the hours when hands grope for love
and dreams for silk-lined coffins,
Saul will plot
how to collect his accounts receivable.
The taste of black blood in the soul.
The king changes course,
decides to stonewall time
hoping fortune smiles and he escapes
without seeing his son betrothed,
and perhaps he too suddenly wearies
of this ongoing family saga,

betrayal sealed in the rock of ages
like coal or diamonds
and the covenant merely a pretext
for judges to upbraid, sinners to repent,
the bride to ravish her beloved again.
Saul does another kind of reckoning:
Jonathan is his son, he is the king,
sometimes royal talent is best employed
to neutralize the enemy
on the battlefield of dinner;
and so Saul decides to say nothing,
instead tells his son to bring his lover
to the feast of the new moon.

*

Like a towel:
darkness on the face of the earth.
And like a goat on a spit:
memory.
Jonathan does not hurry to his bed.
He has learned.
Blood is spilled as casually as semen,
and semen as casually as love.
His father's resolve will not last.
It trembles like a lulav in the evil wind,
and the evil nothing more
than the beat to which he moves,
an urge like that of plants to sunshine.
With his lover it is quite the opposite.
The zig-zag ways hide a lodestar
over which they disagree,
and so David is true but not to him.
If his sister were still here, who knows?
And who knows if she is not?
But all that changes little.
He has given to this man
what there was to be given
unto the lining of his flesh,
and is still content at night

to search for his soul with his sex,
in the morning to open his eyes
on that head of red hair
he takes for the gold of Africa.
And yet a little has changed.
He no longer hastens to give him news
of his conversation with the king,
and when he arrives he too says nothing.
Tomorrow, he figures, will be time enough
to pass on the invitation.
Tonight a nude shepherd
sits propped up against his white pillows
and smiles at him with eyes that could crack wheat.
Jonathan has no choice,
slips in between the sheets
that are soon drawn over their heads
and fold like a tent to imprison love
for one more round of darkness.

In the morning they get down to business.

"I feel as if I've been asked
to attend my own funeral."
Those were the first words, sharp and dry,
to shoot past the redhead's lips
and twist his smile into a new day's bitterness.

"Maybe that's what he wanted
but that's not what he said;
gagged on his anger
and offered grace,
especially after I had made it clear
he has to take us both,
in murder or the breaking of bread.
He said nothing."

Again the twisted smile,
but this time the words themselves
curl into a crooked line
that seeks his lover's bloodstream.

"I tell you, Jonathan, with your father
I am but a step away from death.
Think for a minute what was really said."

And David takes the son back
to a conversation he did not witness.
Jonathan thinks; sees the many faces
of the silence that is his father,
sees the eyes freeze to hide the scorn,
sees the cheeks go soft with love
and then fall into the runnels of habit,
the saglines pulling the mouth down, open,
an oval of regret it knows as home,
but before the words come out as usual
Jonathan sees the king's eyes waver
as if some ghost had floated past
and forced that well known face to reassemble.
The jaw eased up,
the skin at the temple smoothed out,
and Jonathan took as a seal of armistice
this flesh making peace with itself,
but now notes the lips never once
creased themselves into kindness
and so is willing to consider
resignation as a form of revenge.

David leads with an upper right
into this cavity of doubt:
"What have I done," he wants to know,
"except to have you love me?"
Though he knows that is more than enough.
Terrible.
Yet far beneath the choler of a king.
Which makes his question also a cry.
Black as crow it veers into the air,
homing in on the Gates of Heaven
with the two-fisted fury of a little boy,
but Heaven is silent as usual,
and the unopened cry falls back to sender.
David is as startled as Cain

when his burned corn turned God's nose aside.
It is like that with offerings.
They always ask more than you are willing to give.
But this time there was a third party
to a man stumping the country of the heart,
who cast his own cry
into the deaf cupola of blue.

"And don't you love me?"
asked the man who loves of his lover.

"Yes, I love you,"
the answer shot back quick as an arrow,
so quick it went straight through Jonathan's heart
and left not the trace of a word.

*

The children of man and woman
climb from the sea to cling to lovers
as mussels cling to rocks,
and yet they keep on climbing
as if the air were stairs
leading to perfection,
and so are caught
between a lover and the idea of a lover
as the mind gets caught
between a rock and the idea of a rock.
And there,
where the ears have grown sharp
listening to so many words
lull the animal heart,
a man can still forget
and allow himself to think
the little phrase is his benediction,
and think to himself of himself:
blessed is the man in Israel
whose love is returned.
And so Jonathan turned
to the man who would one day write

he has seen the end of all perfection
and said:
"What is your wish that I may do it?"

David, his head always full of plans,
proposed a scheme to sound the king's intentions.
"Let me not attend the king's table;
instead, as the new moon rises,
hide myself in the field
until the holiday is over.
If your father notices my absence,
say I have gone to Bethlehem
for my family's annual sacrifice.
Say also that I asked you for permission.
If the king finds no fault with you,
his silence, as you have said, betokens peace;
but if not –
if instead the thunder stored in Heaven since the Flood
roars in your ears
like God's voice on the prowl for Adam,
know that he is consumed with hate and we are doomed,
for ere long my blood will water stones.
Yet since you and only you
have touched me with the Lord's covenant,
let no hand but your own,
be it even the king your father's,
slay the friend who is your servant."

The cold words froze the prince's heart,
but his mouth sang like a harp:
"God forbid! Do you think if I knew
my father was bent on doing you evil,
I would fail to warn you?"

"But who shall tell me?" asked the military mind.
"Who of all your father's guests
will excuse himself from the table
to ferret me out from my rabbit hole
and read me a writ of murder?
Abner, perhaps? That dog who carries an axe

where another man would sheathe a quill?
No, my love; of all the house of Saul
only you bear me kindness,
only you would rise to say
the man is blameless to a mad king
and that mad king your father,
who must in all his madness
let his unchained wrath descend
on the son who constantly betrays him.
And then what will you do?
How ward off the blows that box more than the head,
that slap the soul most pure, most weak, most given unto God,
and make of a man an enemy easily stalked?
For if you still have legs, prince,
to bear you from that atrium of slander,
be sure the king has eyes to watch where go those legs
all the way to Bethlehem.
And so my lord, my friend,
my soon-to-be-carved son of a king:
when next you come to see your love, bring the knife."

Jonathan listened with all his heart
to despair wrap itself round his lover's veins.
David, he knew, did not do well confined to quarters,
but Jonathan much preferred him here
to being shut up in the hills of Ramah.
In fact, a chicken coop would do
as long as his eyes could open
to a motley of golds
on the haunch that lay across his morning.
So, at least, he thought, as fancy rose
to battle with despair.
But a king's son knows
crowns and courts draw lines of etiquette
to govern the burden of insult,
dropping their do's and don't's
like embroidered napkins in young men's laps.
And Jonathan sorrowed
for his friend's pride that suffered so
it could not bend a knee to love

but bit its lip and played for mercy
to a gallery of dead souls.
"Come," he said and took him by the arm
when he would rather have taken him full body length,
"let us go outside and walk in the field."
And the two of them went into the field.

*

It is always summer
in one of the histories of men.
Shoulder to shoulder two lads walk
happy as they never again shall be,
kicking time like stones, bending now and then
to scoop up pebbles or tear a grass from its bed.
The pebbles they will throw at trees
because their prowess has not yet found
anything worse.
The grass they will stick between their teeth.
They do not know fire separates their bodies,
do not know that light and heat
are God's rules to divide the firmaments,
that when the earth heaves in labour
grief is born in the rock.

For the heir to the throne and his boyfriend
each step into summer hurts.
Jonathan in particular finds it hard
to run his father's wrath again.
He knows rage sleeps in his father's soul
like a well fed snake
only love will rouse to battle,
and of all loves
none but his own so warms the king's blood,
brings it so quick to fever pitch
soon father and son are armies
unto themselves.
In the past he has always held back,
preferred retreat to standing tall
over a blood-stained ground.

Not that he lacked courage
which only redoubled at every skirmish,
but he feared he would one day raise his hand
and bring it down like merciless rain
until he had whipped father and king
and shamed himself
into an exile of no return.
But most of all he felt locked in combat
that would never yield him victory.
And was.
And all for a love that whispered in his mind:
you are a man with only one story
and a single season.
Perhaps; and perhaps for that
he had taken his lover by the arm
and steered him out of doors,
out into that field where they had first lain down
by the rock that stood as sentinel,
nude as the day they were born
though time had grown like hair on their bodies,
and equals in love, slipped into still life.
And perhaps for that too
before he took his lover's arm,
before the word "come!" had even escaped his lips,
Jonathan had decided to see
if this man whose sex he longed to touch
was henceforth going to stay the night
or be forced to leave in peace.
And turning to David in reply
as much to his own request,
gently and firmly said:
"Keep walking.
Eyes that can see to Bethlehem
may not think much of two men strolling in a field.
Tomorrow I shall draw a bead on my father's humour.
We shall soon know if the wind
has truly changed in your favour,
or his heart still bids him gaze
upon your mortal remains.
Whatever God deigns to reveal,

be assured it shall reach your ear.
If the news is bad you shall go in peace
for I shall send you away,
and we both shall wish that God be with you
as He has been with my father.
But this much promise me:
however long I live
do not avenge the Lord upon his messenger,
and when I die
do not remove your mercy from my house
but guard it for that ever I would have kept you,
even past the time your enemies choke
on the dust of your heels."
And thus had him swear, hand upon thigh,
eye staring into eye, God's unspoken name
passing from pupil of ice to pupil of sorrow.
Yet no sooner sworn, David was made to swear again,
no covenant now between one house and the next
binding love to the power of legal documents
but the simple declaration of one man
to another who simply had to hear,
the words a caress returned
like a scroll to its urn:
"Yes, yes, I love you,"
and the words never repeated enough
because he who loves loves to the power of doubt
and his soul embraces
what is not in a soul to embrace.
And yet the words stay the trembling
long enough for love to plot.

"When we get to the edge of the field
we shall enter the run-down woods
that harbour the hare, the raven and the owl
and now shall serve as your city of refuge,
for I alone shall return the way we have come.
But on the third day hence make your way to the stone
where first the deed was done
bringing me forever into the smell of your groin
and lie in wait.

I shall come with my lad and my arrows
as if to hunt,
and as I draw near shall let three arrows fly.
If, when the boy goes to fetch them, you hear me say:
"Here, the arrows are right beside you, pick them up,"
know that all is well and you can come to me
like a cup on a butler's palm.
But if I say:
"Go further, for the arrows are beyond you,"
know that the Lord has sent you away
and all we have said today
shall have nothing to hold it fast
but the kiss of parting and the eye of God."

As Jonathan's lips closed round this warning
the words closed around the field
and swallowed the lovers,
turning two into one as he had said.
And David hid in the woods,
and the king held forth at his table.

*

The moon in the sky, a sliver of bad news.
But eyes on the ground look up and hope
as the smoke rises like a prayer;
two young bullocks, one ram,
seven he-lambs of the first year,
throats slit in homage
to the perennial belief
in commencement exercises:
maybe this month the Lord will stir dread
into the vigour of old bones,
and the buzz in Saul's brain
flatten to the rhythm of a wave.
So Jonathan hopes
as the sweet savour of dressed lamb
weaves its hidden trellis to God,
but his eyes stay fixed
on the bowl of blood at the foot of the altar,

this left
of the animal
who poured out his love
into silver.

Later those self-same eyes watch
as the king takes his seat against the wall
where his spear hangs in its stirrup.
It is not his usual seat,
though a king's seat is where he sits,
and Jonathan remembers his grandfather's mouth
quietly sawing the air:
he who changes his place changes his luck,
and rises to change his own.
Abner quickly lets his ample behind
spread onto the ermine cushion of a prince,
while Jonathan, two seats down and opposite,
sits next to an empty chair
that stays empty all evening.
Like every eye at that table, Saul's takes in
the forlorn space of an invitation refused,
but he does not say a word,
not even when Abner suggests
David is absent because it is that time of month.
The company laughs as company does
when jokes are made at the expense
of those who are safely few,
the laughter even cheaper than the jokes
cutting where the sword fails to cut,
and a man brings to his dreams
what a fallen soldier's soul carries to paradise
when lying guts spilled in the dust
a general's gleaming boot thuds into his belly,
"last call."
Jonathan too does not say a word,
though the faint blush of shame crimsons his cheeks
as sorrow and rage crimson his heart;
the stakes are higher than striking a blow
for principles and their outcasts.
And again the son is bound to the father,

who hopes to himself that David indeed is unclean.

Twenty-four hours:
time for a man to bathe,
rinse his soul free of the body's issue
that keeps him counting his mornings,
and graciously come to table
because the king has stilled the whispers
that run evil to a man's hands
the way the memory of cleft buttocks
pumps blood to the genitals forever.
But though it is the morrow
David's place is still empty.
Saul contemplates the vacant chair.
Is it a challenge? Surrender? Mere bad manners?
He does not know, half of him thinks he does not care,
but the court has already decided
that a seat unoccupied at the king's table
borders on high treason,
and Saul cannot plead ignorance:
the other half urges he is staring at a throne.
And yet he is resolved
the king shall be slow to anger.
The lamb roasted to God swims in its red-stained fat.
Saul's knife spears a chunk that he drops on his bare plate.
His fingers reach for the fine saffron grains
that beckon to be rolled,
obeying the softness that stares at them
as last night the maiden's breasts
stared at him from their softness;
and rubbing one grain against another
his digits remember love.
Thinking thus,
yet not thinking thus —
for sometimes when a man takes a woman
it is only the hands that remember;
how he cupped her and she bent,
how he thought he had slipped beneath her skin
open like a dress at the back
and groped his way past kidney and liver

to the vital organs of her soul,
but it was only her back arched against his sex,
only the sharp little cry of love,
and yet his hands will swear
the laws of science were transgressed –
Saul barely turns to his son
as he puts the long awaited question:
"Where is the son of Yishai
that he has been here neither today nor yesterday?"
And Jonathan,
his heart trembling like a filly in the cold,
answers with the plumb line of the dead
how David asked of him permission
to go visit his family,
for they too were celebrating
the rising of the moon,
and his brother had ordered him home:
"I had not the heart to keep him here
against his brother's wishes,
and who knows if the voice of the brother
is not the voice of the father?
Thus is he gone as I have stayed
to grace the king's table for two."

But Saul would have none of that.
His son's answer was too perfect
to let a king's worries lie,
but so too was the question
as Saul well knew,
knew as soon as it was asked
and last night's memories dissolved
with the haze of good intentions
that make up the kindred of men
whose other coin is fury.
And a shade rose out of Saul
to loom even taller than this tallest of men,
and out of the shade a voice
that silenced the voice in his own throat,
fire become sound as the crown turned to fire:
"Perverse and rotten son,

who crawl along this twisted road
that leads only to the death of kings,
how stupid will you be?
Time and again you give yourself to this Yishai boy,
bless his cunning with your princely love
because you have seen him naked
as if naked were all there was,
as if your mother's weeping flesh
were never heard when you pulled down the sheets
to expose your royal shame.
It never occurs to you, does it,
that as long as you strip this man
whom you so kindly sent to his brother
your own kingdom will never be safe;
indeed, as long as the son of Yishai walks the earth
this palace might as well be at Bethlehem
and you forever a dangling man
he jerks on a string no woman would suffer.
But I will not have it so,
I, Saul, son of Kish –
who came rough hewn to the crown
and put my shoulder to the throne
as my father had taught me to put it to the plough,
so that you and your sons and your son's sons
inherit a land knitted valley to valley
deep-loamed with respect –
will not abide this upstart son of Judah
who has wormed his way into your soul
to grub up my kingdom.
Listen, therefore, son of Saul, prince of Israel,
you who cannot see the difference
between the declarations of war and love:
bring me this man,
for he must die."

Jonathan blanched
and his soul screamed
as these four words pierced its chain,
tacked it like a shadow to the wall
and drew forth white blood.

"But why?" the man cried out
in his last answer to his father.
"Why must he die? What has he done?"

And the son's words thrust in their turn
into the king's temple,
running him out of words
he now knows are futile.
The king in his fury reaches behind
for the spear that draws red blood.
His fingers close tight around the haft
as he balances it in the air,
they too unable to decide
which of love's faces to kill,
and for a moment no longer than God's wrath
remember the infant's dark head of hair,
his tiny limbs and quiet breath
after the battle of the birth canal,
and so the king wavers just long enough
for the spear to be thrown like a slap.

Furious too,
Jonathan rises and flees this table
where murder has been decreed.
Down the corridors he runs
to the one room he can call his own
for the bolt that secures the door,
and there he stays,
unhappy as ever man was unhappy;
for his lover is lost
and he has been shamed by his father.
He goes to sit where once together
they looked out into the garden.
The sky falls into his face
as sad and peaceful as a lake,
blue bruising the world in its war of succession
until at length the crescent moon
carves light into the man's pain.
But to what good, he wonders,
he who knew before they sat down

to the meat he has not touched all day
the risk was high and the odds even higher
that David's absence would draw the king's ire
as an open flue the hearth flames in winter;
who knew even as he doctored the plan
he was sealing his own broken love;
but not this –
not this delirium of a father
who takes to a misdemeanour such royal offense
that judgment is but suspicion cankered
and turns on his twice outmanoeuvred son
the venom of an aged tongue.
Tears steal down Jonathan's face
as a lover scales the dark to his beloved.
For seconds they are caught in the moonlight
and gleam with the smile of silver.
Then they move on,
refugees with their own brand of hope,
and this man who did nothing but love
knows his noble heart is cracked.

*

The yellow world glares like a dictator,
and the eyes stay closed to avoid gazing
on a gaze become insufferable.
In the bed the sheet coils like rope
about the sad, damp body.
Jonathan wakes only with his ears.

A knock at the door;
it is the boy come for the hunting.

One must rise, then,
swing feet onto the floor,
cover one's shame with whatever's at hand
and go and unlock the door
to keep an appointment
made in the days one had an agenda.
Jonathan rises.

He crosses the room to let the boy in.
Someone has to see
how sleepless sorrow wears on his face,
and it might as well be he
who has not yet reached the age of love songs.
He will not be long, he tells the boy,
though hurry is now an outworn measure;
everything rasps,
and the birds that chirp in the leaf-green dawn
are one with the sawing of wood.

When the man and the boy walk in the field
you can tell the day will be pitiless.
The air is clear and sharp
and strips the earth of its armour;
by noon only fools will still be trying
to eke out love from the land.
A slight breeze blows through the boy's jersey.
His smooth chest shimmers with bow-and-arrow happiness.
Virgin nipples, Jonathan thinks,
they know nothing of the kindness of men;
eager to shoot at birds, that is all.
The boy hands him an arrow from his quiver
and he lets fly,
aiming into the bare expanse of blue
at nothing more than a blur,
man-wing against God's:
snap, hiss, the escape velocity of feathers
posing the ancient question:
why did you take me from Egypt
to die in the desert?
And another, and another,
until Jonathan tells the lad
to go and fetch the arrows.
As soon as he sees the boy slow down
he calls out those terrible words:
"Go further, for the arrows are beyond you."

But the boy has no need.
He bends, scoops, runs back to his master.

"You miscalculated, Sire," he is happy
to report, and empties his laughter to the sky.
Jonathan only wishes.
His lips, like a bent hanger, rue all,
even the lad's innocence.
His mind races to the rock
where his lover is crouching
and crouches beside him
to check if blood oozes from his winded soul;
for the lousy directions that sprang from his throat
seemed to part the air like his father's spear
and strike with the guided vengeance
of the law's long arm.
But a mind lacks eyes, lacks hands,
and the stillness in the field is such
as ears are useless.
Jonathan turns on the boy
whose crime is boyhood,
the already airborne eyes,
muscles stretching the bowstring:
"Here, take my archery.
Enough has been shot for the day."
And when the boy hesitates
because his face has been turned away from the future,
bids him make haste and worry not;
there will always be days
when a master kicks life like a can.

*

David hears Jonathan's lonely footsteps
and waits no longer.
Rises.
At once rises.
A diver breaking the water's surface.
A prisoner his bonds.
A wail its sorrow.
And falls.
Three times rises and falls
until the full-length lover has turned

to a howl in the dust.
Jonathan stares like a bronze,
surprised at the derelict hands
encircling his feet.
They knew it could come to this,
would come,
David more than he,
but knowing the future is sometimes
like knowing the past,
the battle dates mere numbers
to reveal a tale of hope and ruin;
one is therefore well advised to sound one's heart
before entering history.
Even a priest listens
before dashing blood against the altar.
But not David,
who picks up people like war campaigns
and figures it all as the calculus of God's grace.
Jonathan does not approve,
has never approved,
has more than once told him he misreads his own heart,
but has come to appreciate
that his lover, like a caterpillar,
only learns by shedding his mistakes;
and so ought not to be surprised.
And yet is.
The man's pain is so great
it cracks the ground on which he kneels
and runs the fault line to Jonathan's heart
that weeps, weeps,
for this poor tumbleweed of love.
It is all he can do to pull the man up.
His cries screech against the air,
are gone,
again rise up,
a mad assault on a sponge.
Jonathan hugs David close,
his lips on his neck, in his ear,
murmuring the prayer for ex-lovers:
"God Almighty, let him not fall by the wayside,

nor rot in despair,
nor spit on hope.
May he remember life is long,
and that I love him;"
and with the hand that caressed him to the tailbone
rubbed the prayer into his bones.
Quiet limped into David's body.
His sobs grew less and turned to tears
that flowed over the prince's shoulders,
wet, warm watermarks of love
that mingled with kisses;
and the kisses soon drew forth an embrace,
and one embrace drew forth another,
until David,
as tradition would later have it,
exceeded.
And then Jonathan sent him off
in peace as they had sworn,
tongue to tongue
and seed to seed
as God was their witness.
And when David could no longer be seen,
Jonathan also turned his back
and returned to the city of kings.

2

Now is life split
into the dark side and the light,
into the almond and its heart,
into the red belly of the watermelon
and its tough green hide;
and the fissure runs right through this land
no thicker than a finger.

Jonathan has retired
to the silks and linens of his quarters.
He will not speak to the king
who must whet his spears alone
on rumours of David's whereabouts.
They are many,
which honours a man on the run
but rattles the lord who pursues him.
"Near Haret Forest, you say,
but a short while ago it was the land of Moab,
and from a family gang his camp has swelled
to over four hundred men;
every debtor and malcontent in Judah
rallies to his banner.
I am surprised you're still here, you fickle Benjamites,
for surely to you will he also disburse
fields and vineyards
and set you captains over armies.
Why else is everything kept from me?
How is it I was last to know
of my son's pact with the son of Yishai,

and know only by deduction,
putting two and two together myself?
Or are you so blind you do not see
how my son now dresses in fine purple,
calls for song, consults poets,
never more touches bow and arrow
as if men's fingers were made to pluck a harp?
He is waiting, it seems, but for what
if not for his lover's return,
for that man whom I took into my household
when he was a boy
and elevated to the rank of prince,
to carry out the plot conceived in their ill-warmed bed.
Thus does a son stalk his father from afar
and you permit it,
telling me everything after the fact
and useless what you tell me."

Saul's servants shrank back
aghast at the accusation:
cabals where there were none,
treason where love,
and feared for a mind so abused
it conspired against its own crown.
But Doeg the Edomite,
whom Saul had set over his company of men
to steward his affairs,
knew this was his chance for tenure
and scratched at the king's wounds;
like every human snake
started off with an apology:
"Forgive me, Sire,
at the time I did not understand.
Not knowing what you know
and little thinking the king could know more,
I kept what my eyes had seen and ears heard to myself;
such is the pride and folly of servants.
But now I fear I have caused you harm
which no late tidings can repair,
and yet to withhold again

what never should have been withheld
only compounds error and disservice;
I pray you, therefore, listen.
By chance I was at Nob when David arrived there
barren save for his clothes.
A man on the lam, I should have thought,
would have were I a priest versed in court affairs.
Instead I only watched, listened,
then buried in my head what men of God
could interpret far better,
and yet I saw Kingbrother son of Goodbrother,
priest to the Lord,
give David bread when he asked for bread
and a sword when he asked for a sword."
But Doeg did not say
that when David appeared at Kingbrother's door
lonely as a beggar,
the priest started and straight away asked
why no man was with him;
did not say he heard David invoke
top secret status for a royal mission,
and when the priest balked
at handing over the Lord's meat,
assure him his men's vessels were as pure as their bodies,
for the king had sent them three days ago
to a rendez-vous far from women;
nor did he say that when David asked
if the priest had spear or sword to spare
on behalf of the king's pressing business,
the priest himself made haste to yield
the only sword at hand, and then retired
to entreat God for Saul's success.
Thus did Doeg withhold David's cunning from the king;
and so withheld, cunning to cunning conspired
to slay a blameless man.

The steward's after the fact report
rang in the king's ears
like the cleaver on a slab
where sits the eager meat.

"Bring them to me," Saul commanded. "At once.
Bring all of them, in fact,
the entire house of Goodbrother,
down to the least of those goodly lads
who would sniff the behind of God."

And the priests were brought and promptly accused
of consorting with the enemy,
and when they protested: 'What enemy,
but the faithful servant of the king?'
sealed their doom with their innocence.
Saul turned to his runners and ordered them
to make ready their blades.
"Surround them," he cried, "and run them through,
for they too are in league with David.
They too knew he had fled, yet said nothing to the king.
As God was their witness, they claim,
forgetting that God has long ago left this court."
But the runners balked as once did the priest
and laid not a hand on their swords.
And Saul turned to the Edomite
who had never come out of Egypt.
"Rid me of these priests," he begged,
"for they are an eyesore even to the Lord."

And Doeg, this erstwhile herdsman,
rounded up the priests as if they were sheep
and drove them into a circle,
round and round he drove them
until the circle tightened on the priests like a noose,
and when the huddle of men had grown so close
even their prayers were squeezed from their bodies like wind,
this Doeg and his henchmen went to work,
hacked left and right at the mass of linen ephod,
and in less time than it takes to regret
had transformed this favourite hillock of the king
into a bog of blood. Red was everywhere.
It ran from dead eyes, from split ears,
from heads severed at the neck and legs at the knee,
ran in crazy lines over eighty-five white tunics

all the way to Nob; for Saul had not forgotten
the hard lesson of Amalek,
had Doeg and his men pursue his vengeance
all the way to the city of priests.
Not a woman or child to be left alive,
not an ox or an ass spared;
the town lifeless, he told them,
and the money left on the street
for the dust to cover.

And so it was.
A posse rode out from the palace
and laid waste the city of Nob,
and for a moment Saul's mind knew peace;
there are troughs in a fever,
deception in the sweet tooth of revenge.
But in Heaven
one of the angels shed a tear
for this king who had got it all backwards:
what God wanted and why,
when and from whom;
words from a time when his kingdom was frail
now used to bring him in line with madness:
to see within
the enemies he could not see without
and destroy them, utterly,
having learned once that pity is unbecoming;
and the angel shook his head
at the gap between God and His creation.

*

First a line of trees.
Then a forest crawling up the hillside.
And then the hills, ringing each other like a belt chain.
Behind, where the brown tops slope into a bowl,
David and his men camp. Voices rise,
slide over the pebbled ground,
chafe against stumps of rock and bush.
Dispute is in the air,

harsh, nervous;
the sky is far too open.

The Philistines besiege Keilah
according to the scouts' report.
David wants to go to the town's rescue.
His men rein in their bravery.
It has taken them months to secure
this mountain fastness, and even then they are wary.
Saul has his eyes everywhere.
Some look out of love, others are on salary,
but to the men it is all the same:
the man on the donkey path who said hello
might as well be saying good-bye,
and the woman who swore love for five minutes
upstairs at the inn
could next move just as easily
to signal the captain of the guard from her window;
she bares her breast for king and country
and the officer gets a hard-on
he turns into a knifing on the road.
In all of Judah they are only safe here,
high above plain, town, even mid-level olive groves;
floor of red dust, thin sheeted roofs,
the backside of majesty.
"But it is not home," David reminds them,
"and never can be without the trust
of the people who now are spies.
We shall need food, weapons, a clothesline of news,
we shall even need love beyond our kin's love.
All that lies in the citadel
we will deliver from the Philistines,
for thanks like a secret fear
now cowers in the tower.
Unless you too are afraid, prefer to wait
in this pen the king has fenced around us,
praying for a miracle
as our throats shrink and the spine shivers
in a hopeless game of patience,
our destiny sealed like farm chickens.

Keilah is a chance that lies before us
like a woman whose hands have loosened the stays;
you tremble, and are right to tremble,
the bodice is about to fall.
We go."

And they went. Rode down the sharp paths
and through the woods and across the burned land,
and fell upon the Philistines in the dry noon heat
when even their cattle found it hard to flee the sword.
Four hundred men cut through their camp like a cage of knives.
The glare of raised metal blinded;
and as the Philistines cried for their eyes
and lifted their arms for shade,
the blades whipped down,
lopping whatever looked to the sun for mercy.
In an hour the field was litter:
forearms, half heads, collar bones exposed
and nibbled by flies. The gates of Keilah
opened to David and his men.

Evening.
Its star pasted in heaven.
Luminous blue. White gold.
Men dream of perfection and settle for peace.
Families, who three days ago were slated at best
for slaves, tonight stroll about the parapets.
And for the same three days
David and his troop have washed and perfumed.
Nor did they forget their horses,
who whinnied their pleasure at coats that gleamed in the dusk,
rich as any master's.

David stepped out onto the belvedere
and with him the leading townsmen,
his chief lieutenants, Zeruiah and his son Yoav,
and Zeruiah's other son Avishai,
golden haired, heart pure,
watching his leader's every move
to learn what makes a man a man

and other men love him.
His red hair glowed in the evening sun like fire.
The rest was battle hardened, supple, daring,
yet sorrow hung from his shoulders. Men worried for him,
thinking he worried too little about himself,
but most feared him, sensing God was close.
Perhaps, thought Avishai, he will never grow old,
and men will always want to touch him.
The Keilah elders fumbled for their words.
David let them break upon their sentences.

"We are grateful – "

"But how – ?"

"When –?"

And answered their unformed compliments
with compliments of his own:
"Your city is well cared for. It would have been a shame
to lose it."

They could not agree more, and again are humbled.
David sighs softly, so only he can hear.
Before him the pink walls
holding children like glasses on a tray.
The elders have not yet offered him refuge.
He wonders if he should ask. And when; and how.
His men are shaven, wear clean shirts,
sling arms around women's waists.
Last night he dreamed of Jonathan.
But the place is so exposed, sits on the highway
like a picnic basket for the hungry.
And Saul is hungry.
He scans the horizon as if it held an answer.
Suddenly it does. The distance starts to swirl,
and a cone of dust races towards the town;
in it fly feet, a tunic's arms pump air,
a black beard slices and bobs until,
in the moat of shade cast by the evening walls,

the cylinder of a man married to the earth
collapses.
David looks down and tries to read the news:
a man's head rests like a flower on stone,
eyes shut upon the world,
his nails dug into the last few feet of hope.
"Unbar the gate," the order slides down the line.
The man is hauled inside,
doctored, revived; and word is sent upstairs
they can call him to an interview. David nods.
His men, like crutches, bear the stranger to the lookout.
A chair is brought. The man sits.
He answers to no name.
Stares through hollow eyes at the sky,
as if more than the pale moon
is hung from the evening.
Slowly vowels form,
the cracked words forced out
in breath begrudged his story.
"I am the last surviving son
of the priest whom David asked for help at Nob.
Saul's men came, dragged my father and all his priests away
and returned only with their fingers.
The fingers they carried in a pail
they dumped in the center of town.
Then they went to work on us.
Wives, children, asses, cows;
whatever moved, sighed, came from parted thighs
befell their swords.
No quarter to treason, they cried,
and lashed and gored and made the air whistle with death.
They hurled infants down stairs, splitting their heads on stone."
Here the man fell silent.
Again the hollow eyes stared past the moon,
stared at an upturned cow,
at dress tatters drifting in the street,
at two legs, wrongly still, aslant some steps:
"They killed our town," he slowly wept,
"tied our murdered souls likes fringes
to a banner they could haul aloft

for all Israel to see.
Because my father was a traitor,
when he was not.
As you well know.
As if that were an excuse."

And David wept to see the man thus weep.

"I should have known," he said, "this country is so small,
men lurk everywhere and tongues are free to wag.
In the shadows of your father's court
I thought I spied Doeg the Edomite."
A glance at the man's face tells all:
Doeg to Saul, king to Kingbrother,
a lethal game when underlings
can silt their master's ear with half a tale.
David shakes his head as if shaking will undo.
Back and forth, back and forth,
'I cannot believe' tossed like grass to the wind,
but all the while the mind believes,
knows,
is getting used to;
his pockets deep and black as the next man's.
"What is your name?" he asks of the survivor.

And the answer: "Evyatar the Priest,"
falls into the twilight.

Sad beyond sad.
A throat inclined to the terrace floor
corking pain.
David sends forth words in lieu of fingers,
prays they will take the man's chin in their grace
and raise his head to the blue that is also silver,
peach, magenta:
"Evyatar,
I as much as anyone
had a hand in your father's death.
I asked him for help as if I were the king's servant,
not his exiled son-in-law,

little dreaming the kindness I played him for
would turn you into an orphan.
It is I should lick the dust
and beg your pardon,
but even that will not redeem
your father from the dead;
and though such seemly contrition
might tilt the world back onto its axis
and loosen for a moment
the band of pain that tightens round your heart,
it will do nothing to avenge
the sullied honour of your father,
nor the Lord he served.
But I, whom that same Lord has spared,
shall live to haul that banner down
and restore Nob's line of priests to a place
higher yet than that from which they fell.
And so, instead of pardon,
I beg you to grace us with your person.
Your presence shall give courage to my men
and I shall guard you with the care
I should have shown your father.
As for the king, you need not fear;
his reach is not as long as he would wish.
God has changed camps,
and they who abide with me shall know
they dwell in sacred tents."

Avishai, watching from the side,
watches how the skilful words slip in
to dissolve the goitred fear and sorrow.
But David is already thinking
they are not safe in Keilah.
The elders who have heard the priest's son's story
will rapidly conclude the obvious:
a city delivered by the son of Yishai
is a city cursed.
The thanks they cannot deny will turn in their stomachs;
and forced to choose between debt and betrayal
they will have to choose betrayal.

Such is the law of kings
who prey upon their own minds:
come morning, legions are dispatched
to shred the peace of other men's nights.

And so in the morning David assembles his men.

Fresh from love they come, kisses stuck to their bristles,
and from sleep that has washed their bodies
of exile's dust.
Some gather in bunches,
others slink off to line the walls;
a few in this makeshift parliament
simply lean against the well,
their eyes staring down at the dirt so packed
David's words bounce off its surface.
Orders like india rubber
hit them between the pectorals,
round, hard,
and tunnel their soft dreams;
their nostrils sting from the whiff of horse dung.

"We have to go."

Feet displace the dirt. The murmurs still in the chest.

"Saul has laid waste the city of Nob
because the priest gave me bread and a sword.
Here they have given us thanks: far more dangerous.
Of course they can argue they had no choice,
it was David or the Philistines.
But now they will be asked to take new sides,
and the king shall expect of them
nothing less than sly obedience.
That is the craft he knows and teaches the country.
The men of Keilah are not crafty
but they are afraid,
and their fear will make them what they are not;
so when Saul and his troops come down from the mountains
they will close the gates of the city,

and their deliverance shall become our tomb."

The murmurs scratch the air.
The softness between their legs now whines
at what it must give up.
Unkind. Unfair.
Their future a career as desert rats
unfolding in this square.
David would have them believe in God
but it is Yoav beards the men;
tall, rough, unshaved, his chest a clap of thunder:
"Men! You call yourselves men
because you stir when skirts rustle by in the street,
yet whimper when told once again
you have to bear arms.
In only three days you've run soft
as the bellies you slide over.
Perhaps you think the king will forget
you rallied to an outcast he'd rather see dead.
Perhaps you think you can bargain with him,
offer this town as Doeg offered him Nob,
and so together put an end
to all this whining to God.
Only God will not retire
without taking you with Him.
The pleasure that today flatters your minds
will tomorrow turn to disgust,
and nothing remain of your manhood
save the heels that kick up dust beneath a dress.
Of course you will be warm
and sleep between linen sheets.
Compared to that, the desert is pure loss.
Yet better our bones cold
than beholden to this king's kindness.
I too say we ride."

And so they rode,
some men spurred by pride, some by shame,
but when the last man had passed through the gate
the column numbered six hundred;

and Evyatar rode with them.

*

Again the story turns south. Act four. Scene two.
David and his men have retreated
to the wilderness of Zif:
rock brown, rock grey, rock to the edge of the horizon.
They move from place to place like lizards seeking shade,
water too,
anxious to avoid the king's eyes,
for the men of Zif have gone to Saul
and promised him David's head:
"We know he is about the land, Sire. Our shepherds
keep coming across their remains. If you drew a line
from one ring of ashes to another
you would see how his band goes in circles:
wadi to mountain, mountain to wood,
like a fox trying to shake its own scent.
Let our sovereign therefore gather his men
and return with us to the south,
for the king's very name shall scorch their hearts
as surely as the sun burns their skin;
and there we shall trap them between two fires."

Saul nearly weeps because his subjects
have shown him pity,
and yet withholds assent;
rocks from right foot to left and asks for details:
a name, a place, the exact spot of his son's
coronation.
And the men of Zif gave him the name Maon,
and told him of a plain so bare that princes come there
to match their falcons;
to the south of the Yeshimon, they said,
where only one mountain dares aspire to God.
And Saul blessed the men,
and he too rode south.

It takes even a king time

to mount an expedition; the men must be summoned,
their sacks filled, the debt schedules renegotiated.
In the meantime, one man working on his own
can move much quicker. Thus Jonathan,
whose spies kept him informed of what the king was up to;
in less than a day he was gone,
in less than seven his lover's prisoner.

"You could have got killed," the redhead chided his grin.

"And so I will one day. But not for the crown.
For my sheets perhaps, for their fine spun cotton that makes
slipping between them so pleasurable.
Or so my young men would have me believe."

Silence then. Each listens to the other's bitterness
seep through love's gravel;
gathering strength.

"What about you, David? What is it like
to bed down on coarse canvas and draw coarse beards
to rub up against your own?
Or is that now outlawed by a military mind
giving military orders?
Perhaps you are happiest here, far from women;
and farther from men who remind you of women
but are not women.
Still:
what do you do with that thing between your legs,
even more with the way it ratchets your soul
until there is no more soul,
only flesh and the longing for flesh
that rises from the crotch like compost?
And then again:
perhaps, finally, you've got it straight,
and your mind bends to strategy:
how to taunt and evade and sometimes strike
deep into royal territory, and then withdraw;
behind, leaving only a name on other men's lips,
praise so silent

it snacks like a spider on my father's brain
until only one track is left
and he too hatches plans,
day in day out broods
on how to crush you to dust.
He has levied another company of men
and soon will be here, lured by the men of Zif
to what they assured him will be your grave.
I did not like what I heard and came to warn you.
Even had they exaggerated,
the lay of the land did not seem in your favour."
Jonathan paused.
A hand rubs moss
and feels the history of grass.
A mind rubs words and feels the future.
For the split second anyone knows
he knows he loves this man;
like all loves, his too is a liquor license,
and he feels himself on the edge:
his mouth will open and the words fall out dark and swift,
and what hung between them like pleated silver will seize,
and nothing shall cross the lovers' space,
clumped and its borders dank;
but he knew too that it could be otherwise,
that the words let fall could aim for posterity
and all the lovers of all time
would remember that Jonathan also loved David
with kindness,
and he too would remember
how in advance he reined in blasphemy.
Thus on the fulcrum of injured love he paused.

"When first I learned you were in the land of Moab
I was content.
It is outside my father's jurisdiction, I thought,
and that will make it easier;
crossing the border will not be betrayal,
more the kind you do
to take a bit of the country out of yourself.
But before I had a chance to pack, you were back.

All over Judah, reports had it,
although I did not see your shadow
except for my boys' description of it
crossing my father's face. Black, they said,
like clouds bringing death, or cut flowers
turned to old iron.
I wondered then why you returned, what brought you back
from an exile where we might have seen each other
to a land where we could not.
And then it dawned upon me,
as if I too had visited the dead:
you missed my father,
the running battle with each other's spindled brains
that makes you both feel so exalted,
like athletes crazy enough
to believe they will outstrip the breeze,
and so much at home,
the one place we can never leave.
You think it's all his fault;
he chased you out and now hounds you
mid the last crevices of his desolate kingdom.
And yet he is the king, the Lord's anointed,
whom the Lord still allows to reign
though no good end has been promised him.
A wicked form of punishment
for a man as finely tuned as Saul;
he soldiers on,
but the vermin already are at work
hollowing out his upright soul.
Why don't you simply wait, you who have nothing to fear,
and when he dies rule? And I shall second you
as I have seconded my father.
There is more to life than being a king."

And Jonathan stopped David with his eyes.

And David stood there, his own eyes dancing,
pores open like the morning iris,
seducer to seducer radiant
in the air blue as a dragon fly's wings.

It will never end, his body thought,
this man will come down from the mountains
and I of an instant go slack;
night lonely, hard pallet,
campaigns honed by cold vows
suddenly warm, and soft as spent love.
"The temperature will soon drop," he says,
and points to the hills, incarnadine,
then to the sky cheating the day of its work.
"We'll be better off in my tent."

And they were:
two men alone, naked, remembering love,
their bodies roll over and into each other,
fingers caressing a wave and the wave flesh,
now round, now long,
now dipping inward like a coastline,
and then of a sudden surprise
at the nearly forgotten;
they laugh, sigh, bleed into the earth
like murmurs on days of worship.
And then it is over:
this silence, this night, the velvet jam of their embrace.

In the dark of space there is light
and a ball spinning on time,
one part land, three parts water.
Twice daily the tide tugs at the land
towing footprints to the sea,
and twice the land returns;
like a woman's smile,
even, triumphant.
And so in the affairs of men:
business goes up and down,
commerce travels the globe like the winds,
even in love there is something
akin to a trade cycle.

David scoops up his share as if it were barley.

"I too was content with Moab.
The king had sheltered my mother and father
and would have sheltered you,
but Gad the prophet would not let me stay.
'Israel is shamed,' he kept crying in my ear,
'her vineyards are fenced in, her fields threshed to their corners,
and the souls of the land are like the land
squeezed in the king's tight fist.'
At first I did not listen. You know how prophets are;
they grab the tail of a dream and whip it into truth,
then hurl it at you like God's voice
fresh from Sinai.
But the men kept trickling in from over the border,
men beyond my tribe with woe upon their lips,
and Gad's voice now could point and name
and waxed in power:
'How long will you wait?' he asked. 'How long sit back
and nurse love's sorrow, and pet that same love's hope
as if it were your mother's soft, caress-worn coat?
Or would you be like Saul,
who sits and frets at a faded promise?
Yet while he broods the civil bonds grow weak;
the poor fear for their stomachs, the kind for their souls,
while those born to the fiercer elements
in defiance flee a mindless throne
and watch with foreign kings as borders crumble.
Thus does Moab gaze
while Philistines hack at Israel's walls,
and yet you stand dumber than Balaam's ass,
grateful to the sons of Balak
for that which costs them nothing.
Generous they seem, as all are
who are generous at their enemies' expense;
but a quick tally would soon tell you
that Israel hurts, and Moab offers succour
to those who would redeem her.
Or did you learn nothing at Samuel's table?'
Thus did he goad me and would not relent,
day after day stung me with barbs
that conjured up the old man's voice:

'a waste of oil, useless brains,
the man goes fast when cautioned to go slow
and now when speed is urged repents;
pity the seer who has given his eyes to the blind.'
I saw before me Samuel thick with sorrow,
the veins at his neck flapping
like lessons in destiny, and seeing thus,
felt God creep into mine;
blue, beholden.
All those years mortgaged to a desert
and now, again, on barren hills alone,
abroad to boot,
and you a prisoner of time as I of space:
was it to this that I was born,
to stretch my days, as once I stretched my courage,
into light that battles a moth stopped on a sad leaf?
You think I hound your father, but think of this:
I paid my dues at all our fathers' courts
and for my troubles was reviled by men.
Smooth, they said, and wily, as if everything I did
was but an afterthought; you, Michal, Goliath
but stairs to a throne whispered beneath girls' shouts.
Yet when I called my victories good fortune
and remanded them to God, the tongues would clack
about the fair-haired boy, who preens himself
on his exception. 'Gingy', they murmured,
as if the colour were a synonym for deceit.
I even heard the cellar winds bear tales
about my lineage: 'From Moab he comes,
through the great-great-grandmother,
wagging his tail like a dog;'
and half believed their laughter.
It made exile feel like home,
but it was not home;
and so Gad's voice called me
to half believe the other side:
purpose to the loneliness of sheep.
the luck of battle,
your father's disturbed peace,
to the way sister and brother

twisted my testicles
and Samuel shuffled my mind;
even, finally, to a kingdom
that may need me for a king.
And so I returned, and so you have found me;
lapsed lover but not in gratitude,
the covenant we have sworn we have sworn forever.
Go in peace, my brother."
And David embraced this man who would be his prince,
but exceeded not.

No time left
to watch the man who carries his ignorant heart
blend into the sand:
there is light and there is shadow,
and the soundless air stitches the minutes together
into war.

*

Saul and his men have descended on Maon
and are pressing:
against the hill where David is encamped,
against the narrow criss-cross of trails
below the sentries' eyes,
pushing the rock up and back
until the only retreat will be
to the open plain of slaughter.
Even at night the king's men advance
like an army of raccoons.
The clan from Bethlehem remembers Egypt,
the roped-in, choking blackness,
but David stands firm: no one falls back
until iron has knocked against iron
and freed shields from those who bear them.
Plague, he tells them, claws first at the mind.
Still, the tents are taken down, the horses made ready.
Escape, if it comes, will have to be swift and smart
and David weighs his options,
but for once God intervenes

and a messenger is sent to Saul:
the Philistines have invaded again
and Saul is forced to choose
one enemy over another.
And so when Saul breaks camp, David follows,
going east where Saul goes west,
and withdraws to Ein Gedi where towers of rock
stand guard over desert and sea,
and in the towers
water spills down from heights,
carving folds in the lining of the hills.
Another country. Refuge for man and beast,
and even the flowers surprised at their existence;
and so mistaken, like Eden, for a stronghold.

The plain runs to the sea like a carpet.
Philistines rise from the south
and cross it like a hot wind,
a mind of its own meaning mindless,
and brutal as fire.
See: armies of legs clogging the roads,
and when the swarm gets too thick
the legs laced to the knees fan out across the fields,
a hundred rows square of human scythe
mowing whatever is green that lies in its path:
wine, grain, even the child that hides in the stalks.
'It is war,' they cry, and mean
a fiat issued from the stars;
and so rip tents, fling women to the ground,
send their groans of pleasure forced
as payment to the heavens.
By now Saul knows what to expect.
He will come to the plain and see smoke
and know it is the embers of rape
rising to the nostrils of buzzards,
and when later they have driven the enemy south
they will come across the remains:
tatters of canvas,
the gnawed and rotting gristle of an arm,
a pot black and lonely in the trampled corn.

And so it is.
Saul has come and seen and driven the Philistines back,
and now sits outside his tent
and surveys his charred kingdom:
black it is,
like rings of cancer on a tree, black the years;
always since the mantle of service fell on him
he has tried to serve,
and always duty fell short of its mark,
the war with Gaza like a war with the sea
and he – and he alone – having to fashion a shield
out of the furnace of Sinai;
send forth his tax collectors of men
and assemble the levy
into pickets the length of the border
and a third again as deep,
watch as the shield broke the Philistine wave
and then itself broke,
and listen to the people cry to him
as he did cry to God:
how long this scourge, and wherefore are you king?

A wheel, then:
as it turns the mill,
the cart,
the jug still clay in the potter's hands,
sometimes only the trace of a circle
in the hungry sand
or the stamp in the priest's mitre
racking the pilgrims to God,
degrees of slow but always the face of thankless,
and Saul deceived by its one-sided lesson.
At length his eyes tire of this landscape of ashes.
He lifts them then,
lifts his entire frame out of the king's chair
and calls his generals over.
"Three thousand more," he orders, "the lean side of stripling.
The Philistines will be quiet for years,
which leaves only the son of Yishai
before the kingdom is secured.

Three thousand men," he repeats.
"Let the new moon not rise twice before I see them."

In two months Saul has his wish.
The choice of Israel stand three thousand strong
before his gaze. He smiles the smile of a king.
The men see broken glass in the sun
and further on, into the future,
the unbroken flow of crimson.
But the lips shine whole and merciless;
it is now, they know, and rejoice,
a king is about to descend into paradise.

*

Ever since men have drawn lines from star to star
the spore trail leads east;
there the wildflower garden,
the speckled light of goldfish in pools,
and the nearby baths where women swim
and stop from time to time to lay their singing breasts
on the water's tiled edge.
But when Saul and his men reach Ein Gedi
there is nothing save senseless grass
and the mock of falling water.
The men do not care: it is wet, and wetness slakes thirst,
dampens the stink, cools the sun-flamed skin.
Like deer in rut they plunge into the water.
Chests open to the sky,
arms like oars, rowing, rowing,
throats stretched like trees;
and Saul hears only stillness.
Desert country. Dumb rocks. And a thousand eyes watching.
Peeled into the brown, arid sage.
Like lizards, thinks Saul, remembering a time
when to him too the ways of animals
were more familiar than the ways of men.
His eyes rove the hills: nothing but sheepcotes,
and silence so total
the mind subtracts itself from the world.

He moves off then, away from his men, their noise,
their easy embrace of wheat and chaff,
his feet picking their way
to the sad huts high on the slopes,
past gypsum, shale, the well covered quartz,
even the chance obsidian that one day will grace
a royal city,
and climbs into sun and wind
as if he would pass them too.
He can't. The sun and wind are powers more royal,
and this king more weary than his bones
turns into a cave;
there in the stillness and coolness
puts aside his clothes, removes his sandals,
rubs oil into his feet:
Blessed art Thou, O Lord,
Who gives strength to the tired,
and lays his body down to sleep,
a moth folding its wings.

Some houses front the road,
others stand back amid the trees,
the difference between people
who think they have nothing to fear
and those who know they do.
Thus are questions repeated
from one generation to the next:
is it better to be bold or modest,
and if bold, then what place pity?
Behind the sleeping Saul two of David's sentries stand watch;
one stays to guard the king's light breathing,
the other runs to report their deliverance,
the news passing up the chain of command
like water sinking into a sponge.
By the time David confers with his lieutenants
they are addressing him as Sire.

Zeruiah is first to speak,
the curls that fall over his forehead
as dark as his thoughts:

"For two years the king has tracked us
and merciless has been his pursuit;
fanatic, really, when you stop to think
how Israel is not safe,
the nation still a stitched together parchment of tribes
and the memory of sin.
It is told that when the children of Israel
rose up against the Pharaohs
we escaped by the scruff of our stiff necks
and the outstretched arm of God,
but though witness to a miracle
we still refused to believe.
Moses did all he could
to seal our faith into an army,
but when we saw the cities of Canaan
fear gripped our eyes and panic our hearts:
it is a land of giants, we were told,
and so we chose to believe,
preferring a forty-year detour
east to the Jordan
where we could skirmish with God instead of men.
And though Moses was never to set foot
in the land that was Egypt's undoing,
he did live to see
Reuven and Gad and half the tribe of Menashe
lay claim to the cities of Amor and Moab
and hear these kinsmen of Israel swear
they would not dwell in their houses
until all of Canaan had fallen to their brothers' sword,
for they also knew
how loose were the bonds of our people.
Even after the land was conquered
we were prone to forget,
brother rose up against brother
in dispute over parcels of earth and love,
whole clans sued for peace
in the bosoms of idol worshippers
only to discover nothing will atone
for the outrage of one God,
and so were forced to sue for peace among themselves.

Jephthah, then, is called to battle
and keeps so to his word
that even when the battle is won
yields his daughter to God,
a vow so fierce that unto this day
the maidens of Israel are weeping,
yet still the vows are forsaken;
and even Deborah's song,
locking the wheels of Sisera's empty chariot
onto the lilac dreams of the hurt and the angry,
was not enough to make of our people a nation.
Who went before Samuel and cried: 'Give us a king.'
And Samuel gave them Saul, son of Kish,
of the tribe of Benjamin,
who never understood how difficult it was
to be a king, and how little prepared
were they who clamoured for a king
to be a realm. The country lacked a spine,
some iron stake sunk into its entrails,
round which white garlands in time would climb
and men send forth their howl.
We would have served, we men of Judah,
but the king did not see fit to ask our aid.
Too close in kin we are
to be the temper of his alliance;
and when our help did come his way,
his thanks slid off the back of his own hand
and died in the muffle of his cloak.
Remember, Sire, after you had slain Goliath
and gone to war against the Philistines
how quickly grace did sour in his rotting heart;
yet even now, when you have been declared
enemy most formal, you pledge our meagre forces
to the rescue of Israel. So acts a king,
who does not let a city perish
for the sake of honour, while he who would be king
puts the axe to the camp of God.
Therefore do I say: Sire, yes Sire,
Samuel chose wrongly. The son of Kish is not fit
to wear the mantle of a king,

and so sleeps disrobed at the entrance to our cave.
By his own hand disrobed, and thus by the hand of God,
Who has placed within His servant David's power
the man who bars His servant from the throne.
Duty commands what interest would commend:
take Saul prisoner."

Crack.
The air itself.
Out of counsel's circle the lash of Yoav's voice:
"Either kill him or watch him go free.
We cannot take him prisoner."
Silence.
The eye stunned. The ear pricked.
Flesh shrinking at the weal to come.
Instead: the soft low sounds of reason
flow over disbelief.
"Father, you said that Israel is not safe,
and you are right. Who better than we know that?
You said that David, far more than Saul, is fit
to be our king. Again right, and again:
who better placed than we to grant you that?
But those very reasons are grounds enough
to dissuade us from your course.
Imagine Saul our prisoner. Imagine then
the uproar. Those who have done his bidding
will fear our revenge. Forced to defend a past
that outlaws their present, they will move to the attack;
cry injustice, drum up outrage
the width and length of the land.
How dare we touch the Lord's anointed,
it surely will be asked,
and men with no interest will feel themselves obliged
to take a stand on the larger question.
Clans will form that cut across
the old clans of father and son,
and the barely forged alliance of Israel
will split like a log under the sharpened axe.
Saul still our prisoner,
the debate will turn from words to arms;

for a king alive, though captive, still breeds hope,
and hope demands its share of blood.
By the time all shall be said and done,
how fit will David be to be our king
and Israel to be ruled?
Therefore I say, no king for a prisoner,
but if we are to strike, strike fast,
and hope that one fell blow will silence all.
The deed done, like all other deeds, will lie behind,
but nothing is for sure.
A royal corpse ill gotten raises questions,
and no one here seems eager
to lay his hand to what the mind abhors."

And yet they all are tempted;
the cold, the heat, the toll
of always being quarry
has worked its way from bone to reason,
and David takes due note as his eyes scan their faces.
He says nothing, lets nothing else be said,
but turns his face towards the exit
and swings his body round.
Then:
one foot after the next walking in his own dream.
His men fall in behind.
He stops, turns, sends them back;
he too, he and he alone.

Before him the sleeping king, for once at peace.
So it was when David plucked his harp:
the grown man slipping his cares,
the boy proud of his fingers' power.
But now they caress a knife,
and his mind is sharp with suffering.
Sees: the king's chest rise and fall,
the bare whisper, the miracle over and over
fluttering over the deep,
and the lips so unfairly relaxed,
that when alert hurl insults for lack of arms:
whoreson! traitor!

the words working up the mind to murder.
Most unkingly.
And yet he is the king.
So Jonathan said. Yoav too.
And both right.
Still.
This shimmer of breath that is Saul
scrolls down his eyes like a book of grief,
and a finger runs down this shimmer
as it follows line after line of complaint
until rage turns cold
and thumb and index are sorely tempted
to snuff out a windpipe.
And yet he is the king.
So said his lover. Remember.
Remember too: this man, the king, is his father.
Thus David.
A free man.
A crab in a trap.
And the hand that caressed the knife now holds it up.
A glint in the cave's half light,
and then gone;
and by the sleeping king, a robe without its hem.

Back, deep in the cave, water drips.
A candle casts its light.
A scrap of cloth lies on a stone slab.
The men, expecting a king's heart, protest,
but David already rues the little he has cut.
They do not understand, nor can they,
not privy to his neck by the window,
the noonday heat on a stone
or fingers crawling out of a shirt;
countless are the interdictions
of a son's face in the father's
And so they murmur, paw the ground
as if their feet were hooves,
and hope vaguely for a spark.
But David knows the least flame will consume them all,
and pounces:

"The first king not yet dead, already would you kill
the man you push as his replacement. And why?
Not because I killed him, but because I did not.
See how quickly blood runs away with itself,
how shed first in thought it cascades down the brain
until corpses pile up
out of all proportion to their reason.
Saul's death, you think, would put an end to all our troubles.
I say they'd just begin. And yet, like you,
to gaze upon his face was all it took
to make my own blood rise and guide my hand
to slit his throat with our indignities.
But tempting though it was, I did refrain.
Not easy, but I did refrain.
Thinking of you, refrained.
And so, do not take this royal rag
as plunder for the king who got away.
Think, rather, of what we overcame:
the base sin, revenge.
Of what we avoided: the high crime, blasphemy."

And thus, as David calmed his men's ardour with his own,
Saul woke and went out of the cave.

But even as he spoke David knew
how half was left unsaid.
how much a lover's weakness had to answer
for the blood still flowing in Saul's veins.
It is like that too,
the crazy things a heart allows
because flesh flows one way to the ribs
and a man asleep on the ground
reminds the heart's master: this way,
and not the many others.
And yet for all the others pity enters the world.
And also this:
speaking, he heard himself speak,
the lining in his voice urge
how even the cut hem was one cut too many.
And David ran out of the cave,

ran after Saul crying, "My lord, the king!",
the chords in the throat in near despair
because this man the words have to lasso
is not getting any closer.
But although the words fall short, Saul hears something:
vowels spinning in the air, the chink of "king" on stone.
God, perhaps, has had a change of heart.
He turns.
A man is running down the trail, his head on fire.
Seeing the king has stopped he doubles his pace,
arms outstretched, "My lord, my lord" jumping from his throat
until he is no more than his own length away.
Stops then and bows; once, twice,
filling the space between head and foot
with his cry now gathered into his breath
like a shiver into a blanket.
The tangle of red hair rising begins to speak
and again David is running,
but the king is now fixed before him
and the running all in the broken glass of his eyes:
"Why, my lord? Only that. Why?
Why listen to all that scurrilous talk
saying David wishes you harm?
Did I not have you in my power today
and did not people say kill him?
But I would not allow it.
No, I said, he is the Lord's anointed,
no one shall touch him, least of all I.
You look stunned, my lord. Perhaps you think
you are still sleeping; but no, it was there, in the cave,
that you slept the honest sleep of a child
while I stood guard and thought: why? why to him, Lord,
is such peace given, dreams no more lethal
than an icy brook, or a woman's fingers
smoothing his hairline at the temple?
And so I cut your robe, Sire.
Yes, look. Look and see,
there, at the bottom, where the hem should be,
and think how it could have been your heart
that my knife sliced from your clothes.

Forgive me, Sire,
but too many nights have I rummaged in the blackness
for comfort and advice, my thoughts circling
round the loop of your royal wrath:
what have I done to hurt you so, what blow
to man or king, to crown or crown's inheritance
that vengeance should so drive you to pursue us
as drives a man whose prize horses
have bolted from his stable?
For whom does the king of Israel chase
but a half-dead dog, a lonely flea,
whose bite is nowhere equal to his malice
and his malice nothing more
than the gyre of a sad brain,
else why should I have spared you?
Does not the ancient maxim say,
evil from evil cometh; and yet my hand was stayed.
Unless in fashion unbeknownst to me
my hand has had its share in some offence,
and for my sins our Lord does use the king
as scourge for my correction.
And yet, since neither you nor I can name the deed
which clamours for my execution,
I would remand myself to God
to settle in His court
those disputes deemed to be outstanding.
For in this quarrel that divides myself from my king,
it much behooves us all
that God be my judge and not my lawyer."

On that the desert snapped shut,
stranding red king against black
in the rising bowl of silence.
On one side, hill; opposite, a yawn of rock,
dirt, wind.
Only now, now that the voice is stilled
and Saul no longer sees
armies of serpents slither out
from beneath the coils of red hair,
no longer sees the crown

torn apart like a loaf of bread
and his son caressed into abuse,
does Saul himself snap to; it is David
stands before him, holding his hem in his hand.
And Saul, like blind Isaac, raises his voice and weeps:
"Is that your voice, David, my son?"
and slowly, slowly puts it together:
"Blessed are you, my son,
for sparing my life when I sought yours,
and even more for running after me
to tell me what otherwise I would not know:
how God put me in your fist that you refused to close.
Now do I know that you shall be king
and the sceptre that today your hand released
shall one day lodge there of its own accord.
But swear to me, as God lives,
that you shall not cut down my offspring
nor blot my name from my father's house.
Thus may it be said of me
what already is said of you:
he found his enemy, yet sent him on his way."

And David swore, and Saul returned home.
But David kept his men
in the stronghold of Ein Gedi.

*

When men make peace they do not know
it comes in the nick of time.
Only afterwards are they grateful,
thinking how impossible it all would be
were the parties still at war
Yet no one thinks how silly
they took so long to end it;
and next time round no one will remember
how every war comes around to peace,
as in the end it must when families start to fight.
But men begin because they think
that what they have to lose

far outweighs the loss that will ensue.
Hope, some say.
Others prefer retirement.

For years now, Samuel has kept to his house in Ramah,
teeth clamped, eyes turned inward,
soul burning like fire inside hail;
but his ears scrape the entire country for news.
He hears it all,
hears the pericardial wart of a king
spread over the land,
black and gathering in blackness
until it enters the bones of men like fog,
evil everywhere and clammy;
eighty-five priests slain like the shudder of music,
a grown man hunting a boy,
the rivers crying with blood
and drying like the unslaked throats of beached frogs;
and from Ashkelon the widows' shrieks,
and from his own heart the rankle of grief,
his two sons still involved
in shady business deals in Be'er Sheva,
still trying to milk the old man's conscience for a loan –
'remember, Father? if only, Father?' –
and Samuel beginning to relent,
thinking perhaps his mask has been too stern,
but then no! no! as Eli's boys
were once again blown to bits in the wind
and Samuel looped back onto the voice of God:
justice is required of every man
and how his sons turn out is neither proof nor reason,
the because of all our acts long ago inscribed
in the creeping mollusc and the dazzling stars
and the later sounds and letters
and the even later Ark:
because I am your God,
because you were in Egypt and left.
Thus Samuel,
mulling over the news in his yard out back,
pulled his cloak about his hopeless soul and died.

They came from across the land.
from Zevulun and Naphtali,
from Gad, Benjamin and Judah,
from the ships of Dan and the fields of Reuven,
from divided Menashe and proud Ephraim,
from modest Asher, from princely Yissachar,
from the twined fingers of Shimon and Levi.
Their last judge had died,
the one who had warned them against taking a king
as others advise against taking a wife,
and one and all they came to bury him;
also to see if the rumoured peace
between Saul and David would hold,
and stood three rows deep to watch his bier pass by.

A murmur. Then a moan.
The mass of silver locks grey now and lifeless,
the beard already frozen
into a monument.
The moan pressed the burnoused bodies together.
Sway. Crush. A robe passed through countless hands
and the gabble of comment beyond cipher;
sharp tongue at the jagged red,
low lament
at the silk soft as pleasure.
So with the simple shroud.
It passes. Men weep.
Surprised at the way anger has come full stop.
Remember a voice that shook loose mountains,
an eye that dressed down plaintiffs with a glance,
the judgments swift, clean, like darts thrown on target,
the target their hearts and so their future.
But now and henceforth silence,
the counsel mute for all eternity,
and all they have before them is his passing.
Their moan gathers strength, grows thick with voices,
like a wave rises and rises
to rear a house of bitters from the deep.
Beneath the blessings sung to God

curses muttered at a corpse.
Above regrets, cried to the deaf air.
And yet the wail cannot forever rise,
crests like the ocean's towers and breaks
upon the white cloth of the dead.
The men whose cry has broken
fall in behind the litter:
first the priest, waving his benedictions,
then the eye-bewildered king,
next his sons the princes, alert lest he should stumble,
behind them the princes who could dispense with kings
but want an army, borders, a lifetime assurance
of peaceful family reunions,
and behind them the clansmen whose lot is to attend.
David is safely in the middle.
The cortege advances on the hole in the ground,
no sound but for the press of a thousand feet on earth
and the priest shrieking to Israel via Heaven:
"Hear, God, Your people's sorrow
that escorts Your servant Samuel to his rest.
We grieve because he was just and the just are rare.
He spoke to us as one who knew the future,
and that because, like all intelligent good men,
he knew how much oracles depend
on a strong memory
and the cross-examination of the heart.
But we who stray no farther
than the fields where we bring our beasts to pasture,
asked for nothing more than what our neighbours have.
Fools, he called us, and we were fools,
and yet he gave us our king,
commanding king and those who cried for king
not to forget the Lord.
But it is man's nature to forget the Lord,
and so we forgot;
and he hacked a king to pieces in atonement.
In his later years
Samuel refrained from public comment;
still we all took comfort
from the sheer fact of his address:

Ramah, the high place,
where God's word was kept in abeyance.
Now a grave yawns where once that word did sit,
and we fear what our unrestrained hands might do.
Because we fear we weep,
because we weep we honour
this man we commend to the dust,
and beseech You, O Lord, to gather his soul
into the dark caress of time;
and may his memory be for a blessing."

Rarely in these parts does it snow and yet it does,
and when it does the snow falls softly,
dusting men's hair, putting weight on their eyelashes,
wrapping their shoulders in cold cotton.
If it stays on the ground long enough
their horses kick as a shiver climbs their legs,
and what is soft stops the blood and freezes song.
So the priest's words
falling softly and cruelly as snow
into hearts as open as the grave;
they lodge there like ice,
the time it takes to lower a body
into its final trench.
Then the mourners pass,
one by one grab the shovel
stuck into the mound of freshly dug earth,
and one by one toss a clump of dirt
back to where it came from.
Thump! and again thump!
the dull sound of falling books
as the clods hit Samuel's chest
inert beneath the linen gauze,
and mount and mount
until a sod pile century-high
buries forever the once warm sinews of a man.
And one by one the living slinked off to life,
the crown, the mitre,
their retinue of flesh like a bridal train,
even the two lovers

who had to make do with a wire of love
stretched across the funeral throng,
the one turning left
to follow the tremor of his father's shoulders,
the other turning right,
his face set toward the wilderness named Paran.

The sun declined behind the hills,
the newly turned rectangle of earth
slept like the wind in a dream;
and the olive tree, like an old servant, kept watch.
Such loneliness.
Such terrible loneliness in a garden
that only night absolves,
drenching the garden and its grave in darkness.
Then comes day and then again night,
the relentless succession of hours
claiming their inheritance;
and every death an invitation
to step over the line.

*

High above a canyon
the sun like an oyster on fire.
Below, between the hanging sheets of dust,
men eat the yellow wind;
beyond their tents the drowsy camels sit,
eavesdropping like spies in a bar
on news as listless as the air.
David watches his men sink into boredom
thin as the stream that flows through these desert walls.
He has let his beard grow.
It ripens in the sun like tomatoes
of its own wilful accord;
running to the unkempt, you might think,
when men in lazy sport
toss half-aimed javelins into the sand
as his men do,
but the figure that stands in his tent awning's shade

is not unkempt.
Wretched perhaps, and yet a royal kind of wretched:
charcoal in his face ablaze,
eyes above the glowing red as pure and bright as noon,
as love,
as a mind that looks at stone and thinks of prayer.
He calls Avishai over.
"What news, son?"

And the young man answers, proud there is an answer:
"That man, Naval,
who owns enough flocks to feed our entire camp,
is shearing his sheep in Carmel."
And then, fearing the name calls nothing more to mind
than one more master at turning goats into gold,
hastens to add:
"He's the one whose shepherds we befriended
when they drove their flocks of thousands through our hills.
Hoping to avoid the long route, they said,
but afraid of robbers and ignorant of the wells.
Show them the way, you ordered, so they don't die of thirst,
and stick close, in case the neighbours get ideas
about helping themselves to lamb stew.
They did not lose a kid.
Our men were their banners by day and by night their eyes,
and they crossed the wilderness
like a parade down a highway.
They say that virtue is its own reward, sir,
and it is;
our men were glad to do a job and do it well,
and when the last of their flocks
left our brown hills for the green,
each man yanked the bridle of his beast
and rode the sky for home.
But now our men are bored and hungry for fine food.
Surely it would not be beyond all justice
to send a delegation to Carmel
and ask Naval to remember
the servants who helped his own;
for since the wool they lay by is their master's fortune,

they do eat well at shearing time."

David smiles. The smile cracked his face.
Lines crept in at the eyes, the lips pulled up,
life resetting a mask.
It glows.
Windburnt.
Ochre.
And like the desert it too has slipped outside of time.
Forever:
the smell of sheep, his brothers' gleaming teeth,
a knife in the air and an arm that comes down quickly,
grunt, swear, the others laughing
when a ewe makes good her escape,
and rising to their nostrils
the sizzled fat of roasting lamb.
And also forever:
Jonathan's eyes at the funeral,
the eyes that had turned his body to foil
and now turned it to stone,
and he wanting the eyes and the owner of those eyes,
banished by his tongue and he to his tongue beholden.
And so also, out of time, forsaken,
like the old man seeping into earth.

His face reassembles,
the many tiny squares of flesh
now a life mask bent to purpose,
and the smile slightly raw
turns to the young man waiting for a word:
"They do eat well at shearing time,
and so should we. Take ten men
and pay Naval a visit. Greet him in my name.
Wish him peace. Nothing but peace, say,
just as we gave your shepherds in the desert,
and add how glad we are
to see the wool pile up like coin.
God smiles on Israel and on His servant Naval.
It is different in the wilderness,
where God is at home and walks about

naked as the wind.
His smile sears the eyelids of your soul
and nothing piles up save sand,
and men whine like the night longing for the day.
I pray you, therefore, for the son of Yishai
and for his men your servants,
spare a tenth of what you give your own,
that we too may feast and thank the Lord
for returning a favour with a favour.
This say to him, Avishai, and hope he understands
we need sheep and goats more than prayer."

The men gallop off,
digging their heels into their own ambition.
David, watching, has doubts about their embassy;
men are fickle and strangely stingy.
Still, he thinks, let them ride
and make it known in Israel
that the man who lives in the wilderness
keeps a ledger;
and though for the sake of peace,
and his word,
and the man he thought he could do without and does,
he keeps his profile low,
it is best that no one seriously believe
he is above calling in his debts.

Freed from boundless space, his men rode hard.
Like an arrow rode, feathered tips blurring in the air,
and straight as a message.
They came upon Naval eating with his shearers.
Picture the tables set end to end
in the middle of a carpet of fleece;
from one end to the other cruse upon cruse of wine,
rounds of bread, shanks of roasted lamb,
on either side a motley crew of men,
some hewn from rocks, others with faces as kind as babes
lifted from their mothers' wombs,
their robes like a wave of indigo,
their laughter like the roughened hands

that raise a naked body to its cry,
and over this near drunk line of beard
a man swimming in his lordship
like bloated figs in a jar.
Avishai and his men approach, salute, ask to be excused
for interrupting. Naval's men look up.
Some salute back, instantly remembering.
Others, affable by virtue of the grape,
extend an arm in general welcome to the world
and so to David's men; who, for all they know,
may well have crawled straight out of the sky.
But many, Naval included, say nothing;
stare at their intruders and wait
for the words to tell them
why their banquet has become a frieze.
Avishai takes up the gauntlet of their silence,
enters it and breaks it
as deftly as a bird scores the azure.
His mouth moves quickly now, pouring forth the story
David has instructed him to tell.
The story is short, soon ends,
and the mouth closes humbly on its request.
Naval can only drawl:
"Who is this David, son of Yishai,
that I should take of my meat and wine
and give it to a bunch of strangers
who claim to be his servants, and he mine?
You tell your story well, I grant you that,
but the world is full of stories;
every day I hear of servants fleeing their masters.
Perhaps your David is such a one,
comes to me an outlaw half to beg, half to extort
what rightfully belongs to these men
who put in long days before sitting at my table;
men I know by the shekels they cost me
and those their labour brings in,
unlike you, sir, who would hardly weigh
upon such scales of justice.
But since you speak to me of peace, go in peace."

Dismissed.
A thousand waves brimming on his eyelids.
Avishai rolls them back.
Whirls.
Is gone.
Rides and rides into the night he prays will always
stay night.
Races the horses against the motionless hills,
their long legs eating up the garrigue
as he would have them eat up his outrage.
The moon slips by in silence,
beneath the moon his men as wordless as shadows,
and he ahead, always ahead,
a cry haemorrhaging inside him.
They stop at every well, drink, rest,
man and horse alike listening to the air.
Sand, they know, breathes; so does night,
and the idea of night
that lies beneath the darkness they can see,
and they listen to it all
for the sound as subtle as a click
of pardon entering a soul.
No click. No pardon.
Only the stone wells strung out like a line of cairns
they follow into sunrise,
and at the end of sunrise David outside his tent.
Avishai dismounts and is already running,
his running limbs already talking,
and when he gets within earshot
Naval's insult pours out in a recital,
word for word.
David listens, nonchalant at first.
He has heard it all before,
the words as formal as an invitation
declining your request,
no fixed as firmly in men's hearts
as the boulder cross the way that has not moved for days,
for centuries perhaps,
a lone and stubborn rock atop a cliff;
heavy, he has come to realize,

and sometimes red, miraculously red,
drawing the eye it misleads.
But as Avishai talks he hears a new tone
creep into a man's refusal,
and his eye sees a sneer across a face.
"Get your swords," he tells his men.
"We have to teach this man a lesson.
He thinks his men work but mine do not,
thinks gifts are fine that come his way
but cries extortion when those who gave him help
ask for help in return;
and then, to be kind no doubt,
allows we may simply be
hard up coves come to beg.
Who is David, son of Yishai? he asks.
We could have said
the man who when a boy slew Goliath,
but now our swords will answer
and sing another tune."
And adds, half astride his horse:
"God protect Naval; for lucky will be the man
who by tomorrow's light
is left to piss against a wall."

And God,
who likes to listen in on what men say
when anger wags their tongues,
protects him.

*

It is said that God is One,
and even at the ends of the universe
oppositely charged particles are not out of touch.
Thus, when David whipped his face toward the north,
a woman mounted her ass and headed south,
her lips softly closed beneath a veil.
Yesterday one of her husband's men
had come to tell her how Naval
spat in the face of David's emissary:

returning wrong for right, he had said,
nasty when he should have been kind,
"for those men had been as kind to us
as though we had been their brothers,
and now – ;"
and now, she knew she would once again
have to make amends
for the man who swilled feelings like wine,
who even when he took her
was bawling out orders in a warehouse,
his large arms groping
for the life he knew only to devour.
And so Avigayil got busy with her pots
and set her maids to work.
The ovens fired all night with bread and fig-cakes,
the sheep howled when slaughtered, then seasoned in silence,
and while busy hands prepared the mutton
others filled boxes with raisins, huge gourds with wine,
sacks with rushing corn,
then loaded the side dishes of penance
onto the backs of waiting donkeys.
And of all that not a word to her husband,
who snored away the night upon his bolster.
So it was that when the sun cracked the blue sky white
a woman regal upon an ass
descended into the wilderness,
before her an escort of men
bearing gifts as if to a marriage feast.

From light created out of darkness, sky.
And out of the sky, a covenant.
Out of the covenant, love.
That crawls along a road with all the rest.
beetles, thorns, weeds, the cast off stones,
and no more intent.
For hours now David and his men have been riding,
the dust their horses pound
swirling about them like flour.
In the distance at the top of a cliff,
a group shrunk to a dot:

one woman, five men, twice as many beasts
picking their way into history.
Slowly.
So slowly they barely seem to move.
The eyes in the column of dust cannot make them out.
But they see the column, if not the eyes,
and Avigayil knows what it is,
and who,
and cautions her men to wait
in the covert of the hill she rides down alone.
At the bottom,
where the hill crawls away from itself
to unroll into another,
she halts.
And waits.
She and the ass she rode on
waiting in the fugitive light,
the day broken on its hours,
the amber air cracked into dust:
voiceless, soundless,
the stock still moment after bodies were one
and the sex that has wrapped another
sure in its quiet triumph.

From the back of the hill opposite
the clap of horses' hooves,
and then the hooves themselves
burst upon the muleback woman,
forelegs rearing high as the riders pull on the bit,
the pace suddenly broken,
the gallop that runs from the ground to the ear
turned into a terrible whinny,
and the men's eyes wide with the whinnying.
For the moment all has returned
to the first and great confusion:
the rider one with his horse and both one with their cry,
and their cry like a ring of fire
that whirls above their outraged necks,
whirling the blood of man and beast
to leap into the sound.

But the men do not succumb.
Their fingers tighten the reins,
jerk and jerk again:
no horse shall jump through the snarl.
None does.
And the proud heads are bent back toward the earth.

So deathly still of a sudden.
A snort rips the air. The lead horses turn,
shadows on a sundial. Those behind step back;
like wedding guests, careful not to crowd the aisle.
And so a path is cleared, and David rides down:
red rock hair, cinder eyes,
heart bitter as an almond.
Unlike his men he is not surprised
a woman blocks their way;
the land here is bone, pelvic,
and breaks you like a woman's fingers upon your soul.
She wants something, he knows,
no one sits so quietly for so long;
and eases his horse on,
past the last and first of his men,
into the quiet.
Avigayil knows at once
he is the man she has been waiting for,
and thinks: "Careful, now,
he hungers something fierce,
and in his hand your husband's life
as humble as an egg."
She slips quietly to the ground,
bows and bowed she stays
until he too is obliged to dismount
and bring his toe level with her nose,
and even then she will not raise her eyes
past the sandal straps at his knees,
forcing him to bend to raise her up.
But she does not rise,
wants something more than pity or unease
to flow to his heart,
and with the instinct of that woman

long ago in the garden,
clasps herself to his legs,
letting the words rise in her stead:
"My lord, you chase after the wrong man;
nay, even after the wrong sex,
for mine is the fault
and not that idiot of a man
who would be my husband's.
He is as stupid as his name,
forgot as usual to let me know
we had visitors,
thinking he could take care of it all,
even of that which does not concern him.
Had I but known you may be sure
your men would have received their due;
but I did not know, and because I did not know
my lord is prepared to sully his hands
with a fool's blood."
And bringing her own up to his knees,
and her cheek to press against his thigh,
whispers for his ears alone:
"And so himself become a fool
rather than praise God for sending him
such enemies."
And louder now:
"But I do, and praise Him yet again
for staying my lord's hand
until your handmaiden could put together
her simple benediction.
Thus do I entreat your noble heart:
half-way up the mountain
my men wait with victuals for yours.
Let them go relieve us of our burden,
and eat and drink that they may know our thanks
and I your pardon."

But David does not answer, gives no order.
This woman plies his heart; it does not bend.
Nothing in him does.
Head to foot he stands consumed by rage,

and underneath a palisade of hurt;
his mind locked into insult and how to avenge it.
Circle. Wheel. Rack. The round and round of words:
"Evil for good...The morning light...
No one left to piss against a wall..."
And what there is of God is mobilized.

Avigayil holds him tighter,
her voice slipping like a serpent past the marshalled host:
"To what avail, my lord, this clinging to revenge?
To show to all Israel what all Israel knows,
that the Lord is with you and one day shall make you
ruler of us all?
Wherever you go His favour shines on you.
The people see that and rejoice,
thinking of the days when the king's fortune shall be theirs;
and in the meantime turn their hope to maidens' praise.
Can my lord, whom God so blesses, be less patient?
Or would you have them dread the moment
when your foot climbs the first stair to the throne,
all those years the memory hugging their brains:
how quick you were to whip life from that man
who could be no better than he was,
and you not yet the king?
And so for my mistake,
the hosannas that should greet your coronation
will choke on each man's fear of his own vice.
Forbear, my lord," – and the plaint in her voice
drew the ache from his heart – "for even if my words
proved to be the raving of a wife,
my conscience could not bear the thought
that once the house of David is established,
any knave could reach into the past
and fling against the blazon of the king
the worthless blood he once so rashly shed.
Therefore I implore you yet again:
stay your hand,
and wait.
God does not forget the man who walks with God."
And her fingers grazing his thighs,

and her lips brushing his ache,
and her heart weary from her own words, adds:
"And when the Lord remembers you, pray remember me."

A man stands on a beach, at his feet a tree's remains,
driftwood blanched and scrubbed by the sea
and buffed by the wind.
So he, the hurt sucked like rotten marrow from his bones.
"Wait," she had said.
And he: "Why don't you wait?"
And David to himself
noted only the smooth surprise,
as happens when the sea recedes and the wind dies down
and the battered sand discovers it is loved.
But David to Avigayil said:
"Blessed be the God of Israel
Who sent you to me,
and blessed be you who stopped my mind from murder."
And bending to raise her doubting body up,
leaches his own kindness into the eaves of her soul:
"Tell your husband he owes you,
for had you not so swiftly acted
surely Naval and all around him
would not have lived to see tomorrow's dawn
taint their precious jewels a rosy hue.
Then tell him he owes me also.
Still."
And lifting her face to see his own
crinkle into a smile, asks her if his men
can partake of her gifts.

Abigayil, wanting nothing more than this request,
graces his kindness with her own; demure, fleeting,
a kitchen joke kept close to the tongue.
Her lips part slightly, then shut. She motions him
to follow. Up the hill she shouts a word
and soon a train of donkeys ambles down the path,
their backs swaying with the excise on her suit;
and while below David's men hastily unload,
unstrap the gourds, break apart the bales,

hail to the sky the sweet savour of a feast,
the suppliant and the man whom she petitioned
confer like queen and king
in a realm of purple thistle.
And so for a moment they are:
out of time, out of men and women's gaze,
sitting in unexpected sympathy
like a couple in the doorway of a tent,
and in the distance clouds cutting lines in the sky,
like vows and wishes criss-crossed in a hand.
But not for long;
the shouts of men quickly climbed the air
as if the voice, and not the arm,
brandished the dented bone,
and David too rolled the woman's caress
into his throat:
"You see, I listened to what you had to tell me,
and everyone is happy.
Go, then, to your house in peace,
and be assured I shall not forget."

And so Avigayil went home.
But as she approached the house
the sounds of revelry rose from the open window,
and drawing near she saw that in her absence
Naval had organized a drunk:
in the middle of the table a roasted lamb,
heedless knives carving away
while other hands rolled fists of barley onto plates,
and jugs of wine passed from guest to guest
as if suspended from a clothesline.
Every gape was open; some to swill
the crimson liquor, others to spit forth
some ill-turned joke. In a corner
bones had started to pile up,
and already one man's face was sunk in lamb grease.
Behind the men the maids were in attendance;
half in fright, half in too good humour.
Avigayil, no sooner in the door, dismissed them;
and when Naval raised his reeling voice in protest,

dismissed herself as well.
Thus did a husband celebrate
what his wife had come to tell him
and told him only in the morning,
as he stood against a wall to void the night's excess.
The news all in all was good, she thought,
but what he heard froze his blood
and in ten days
had turned his heart to stone.
When David heard Naval had died
he sent a man to Avigayil
to woo her with these words:
"Because of you it was not I
who made you wear the widow's veil,
and yet I had a hand in this affair;
fool of sorts to have sought your husband ill,
but not so fool as not to see the skill
with which you weave the net about the fly.
Therefore in part to make amends
but in greater part to please my hungry eye,
I seek to join your hand to my affairs;
not of great esteem when now compared to yours,
but destined in the course of time to prosper,
as you yourself admit.
And then there is the rest, properly unspeakable."
Avigayil weighed the unspeakable,
and thought it best to have a man
whose feet she would be content to wash.
And so again mounted her ass and pointed it south.

*

An evening breeze, for once.
Reed scratching on parchment.
David in his tent tries to write his love a letter.
"Dear Jonathan," he starts as usual,
but the words look wrong,
and he wonders which greeting is right for betrayal.
And yet the man is dear; dearest even,
more loved by him than anyone

who strays upon this earth.
"By now you may have heard the news.
It travels so lightly in our little country.
I'll spare you the details of time and place
and what each of us wore,
quite certain that what detains you
are the twistings of my cracked heart.
Yes, I went and took myself a wife. Another.
No, Michal was fine. Eminently suitable.
But as out of reach as you; and like you chained
to your father's doghouse.
I nearly killed her husband.
She came to plead his cause as you did Saul's.
Pleaded well, as does everyone
who uses your arguments.
Still, my beloved, I have a question:
for someone so saved, how is it I feel so bereft?
I sent her home to tell her husband
he was secure from danger,
and the man died from fright at his own ignorance.
I waited a decent interval and sent for her.
She came.
She has a name. Avigayil.
She also has brains. And wit.
And something of your sister:
how a throat laughs happily in the long-legged night.
You will say once again
I am never content with the happiness I have.
What is a hut of fleece when weighed against a crown?
A wife given the chance of two?
Or a boyfriend when stapled to the sky?
This is an old dispute between us,
so let me say this in my defence:
perhaps my nature goes against nature's own,
but what true one is there
save the way we softly pluck our loves
until our hands reach for flesh and close upon air?
You said, "Wait."
She said, "Wait."
I wait. Stand aside and watch

the strange ways in which God deals with men,
and think it not so strange
that He may lift the needy from the dunghill
to set him among princes,
or make a barren woman fertile
that she may keep house for a roost of children.
And if all this,
what can we do but praise the light
as I do you, always and forever?
O my beloved, I miss you so;
my tears are like the hyssop's,
and my longing like polished cedar."
And signed his name:
"David."

Jonathan at the other end,
the unscrolled letter in his hands.
He reads it once, twice, many times again:
his friend's words give him pleasure
but do not add up;
the tears in his eyes are his and his alone,
and like nettles sting his soul.
The news itself does not surprise him.
It had already reached the court,
and Saul had lost no time
giving his sister to another man.
Now this; and Jonathan could only conclude
there was nothing left for him to do but marry.
And so within the year
a son was born to him
lame of foot.
But since news does travel lightly in their country,
David quickly heard how he himself was twice divorced;
and within the year married again,
this time to a woman
whose son would rape his sister.
And thus before the old man's bones could rest in peace,
everyone had crossed the line
from Dan to Be'er Sheva.

*

There are days when anger rides the blood currents,
and the brain heaves with one more offering,
and the light that gleams, fierce as dog teeth,
beyond the damasked curtain
makes men forget how noble it is
to stay at home.
On one such day the men of Zif came again to Saul,
and again dangled before him
the promise of David's corpse:
"He is returned, Sire. Our men have sighted his
digging in for winter in their usual redoubt,
there where once your royal fist
was set to close about his throat
and would have but for the kingly duties
that called you to our borders.
Things are different now.
Our frontiers quiet. Our enemies subdued.
The king's house looking toward its future.
And Samuel's warnings become an old man's pique.
Why suffer, then, this desert upstart
to roam about the realm,
his every shadow cast upon a rock
a reproach to the crown,
silent and stubborn as the dead?
Has Saul not done enough to merit thanks?
And what is thanks if not the nation massed,
ten thousand voices' praise for this southern peace:
out of the roar, song; out of the many, one;
the sound itself as brilliant
as a mirror in the sun,
and foil to the king's escutcheon.
On a shield so white no scarab should be crawling.
Let the king therefore act as the king he is
and descend with us to the desert
to flatten a beetle against a rock."
And Saul, still smarting from his children's wounds,
saw a black insect
on the ensign of his newly ordered house, and agreed.

And so again:
three thousand knees crunching the air, left, right, left, right,
like all armies
snapping the peace of brush and stone
and the heat that curls about an afternoon nap.
Thus a king's pride:
a nation massed,
an anthill on the move
sloping down the hills that slope to the wilderness;
but at the bottom, where the land turns to shale
and the endless horizon is baked into the plain
and the river is no wider than a finger,
the chain-mail of soldiers comes to a halt
and the rings revert to men
who dig holes, set up tents, cook food,
wipe sweat from their brows and disbelief from their eyes,
and when their spears in the sand can point to the stars,
circle the king, that the camp may fold in sleep.

All this David watched from afar,
a man with many pairs of eyes
and every one needed,
since Jonathan this time stayed at home.
And so it was
that when the king laid his head upon his bolster
David knew,
and sheltered by his caravan of spies
crept up on sleeping Israel,
the young Avishai at his side.
Together they looked down on an army at rest:
in the center a king, near him his trusted guard,
and spiralling outward a camp so deep in slumber
that the ground on which so many soldiers slept
rose and fell like the lungs of a single man.

"Drunk!" Avishai whispered.

"No. Simply tired; from so much effort
spent to wicked purpose.

It dulls even a mongrel's wits.
Look at Abner, usually so quick
to sniff out danger. Now he's only dead weight,
and plenty of it."

Avishai, bold by nature, grew bolder:
"And there's the king, his spear next to his head
stuck in the ground.
I could steal down and with one blow
affix it to his heart."

David smiled to the darkness, but aloud said:
"And have me watch Abner drive a stake through yours?
No thanks, my friend.
Remember: the king is the Lord's anointed.
When God destines Saul to die, he shall die;
whether by cold, battle, or mere old age
I do not know. Of one thing, though, you can be sure:
it is not my hand shall fell the king,
nor that attached to any of my men.
But this you can do, which better suits my plans:
go to the king's bed but do not disturb a stone,
pluck his spear from where it stands
and take the cruse of water by his pillow,
and in God's silence bring them back to me.
That done, we are surely saved.
Even the king,
though only from murder."

Avishai did not need to be asked twice.
For this man,
who balanced so many futures in his eyes,
he would ride the scapegoat into the desert.
As it was, he only had to pick his way
through a sleeping enemy. Countrymen at that.
But David prayed this escapade
was not his destiny.
And prayed again when he came back unscathed:
"The Lord is my rock and my refuge,
my shield and my horn of salvation.

He has enlarged my steps under me,
my feet have not slipped.
I have not gone down into the pit,
nor he who is my companion.
Praised be God Who watches over me
from His high tower.
Let my enemies be ashamed,
and their lying lips be dumb."
And taking the royal insignia
of spear and jug,
David and Avishai withdrew to a distant hill
where no javelin throw could reach them;
then just before the sun rose to kill the darkness,
David's voice cried out across the gulf
that kept him from the king:
"Abner!"
But the king's captain only half-opened his eyes;
his shades kept their snares about his dreams,
the world filtered through his name
still penumbral teal.
And so again:
"Abner! Abner ben Ner!"
until the shades fled underground
and the teal turned to silver.

Now too much awake, Abner shouts back:
"Who are you, who calls out to the king?"

And David, his voice like honey around a knife:
"I called not to the king but to his captain.
You are a man, are you not,
reputed without an equal in the land.
How is it then, you guard the king so poorly,
and let any jackal bent on murder
approach his royal person?
For negligence much less than yours
men have been devoured
by the fire of God's pan.
Or have you perhaps forgotten
that the king is the Lord's anointed?

This night a man has stolen close to your master.
See where the king's spear ought to stand.
Look for the cruse of water
that sits by his sleeping head."

Abner looks, finds empty space,
his face turns white as lime in a grave;
but before more words fly to slit his throat
the king himself stirs
and rifts the desolate air:
"Is that your voice, David, my son?"
His own voice sad, remembering
sin as sharp as the fragrance of peonies.

Sadness of another kind responds:
"It is mine, my lord,
obliged to interrupt your sleep
and call to my king across a distance
others would gladly see increased ten thousandfold.
And all for what, my lord?
What have I done, what sin committed
that you pursue me thus?
God Himself would long ago
have taken a ram in exchange,
but daily the cursed lips of men
pour poison into your ears.
Traitor, they doubtless call me,
hinting how much I covet your throne
when nightly it is all I can do
to find a haven for my head.
One day they shall drive me abroad
and then tell you how I worship other gods.
Mercy, o my king;
do not I too have title
to a plot in Israel's vineyard,
or shall my life be spent
as a partridge hunted in the hills?
Besides, what good can it do my lord
to see the blood gush from my windpipe to the ground?
No more, surely, that it could ennoble me

to hold your sacred head between my hands
and break all the tendons in your neck.
The Lord this day once again placed you in my power,
and once again I saw to it
no harm befell the crown;
for though you be a king, Sire,
you yet when fast asleep are still a child,
his soul pawned to the moon.
Thus in the common basket of our dreams
your life grew dear to me,
as mine, I hope, shall be to God;
and let Him save me from my sorrow."

Saul wept inside to hear these words,
and his own trickled out like gruel:
"It is I who sinned, son.
I was a fool, and erred grievously,
though it was a king's error;
and so shall it be a king's pardon.
In all safety you can return,
no more shall wicked counsel excite my blood;
and blessed, David, may you be of God
to do great things and prevail."

And David answered:
"Let one of my lord's young men come and fetch his spear
and justice thus return to every man;
and may faith grace the king."
But David did not return;
and again the king and the man he called his son
went their separate ways.

*

Grass runs up to a beach and stops,
as if beyond a certain line
green is excommunicated.
Cliffs rise from the sea and break off just as abruptly.
There is the firmament above
and the firmament below;

those that fly and those that swim,
those that walk and those that slither on the ground.
And all the divisions are named
in declarations of peace and war.
Father and son.
Man and woman.
Thou shalt.
Thou shalt not.

David is lying on his back
and conversing with the stars:
"Saul says he won't but he will. He always does.
It's not just the wicked counsel and the vicious tongues
but the rot that festers in his heart.
Of course it's nice to hear him be contrite.
I'm even tempted to go back and play the harp.
But it's all talk, his as well as mine.
And yet there is some truth to what we say,
only not enough to guarantee my skin.
And then there are the others.
Avigayil. Achinoam.
My six hundred men.
Their wives and children and sometimes more.
Too much to be resolved by promises.
Better, then, to remove myself
from the compass of Saul's eyes,
and hope that in the absence of his quarry
the king will turn to more pleasing pursuits.
Wait. Simply wait.
And see if the old man's labours
bring forth his future."
The thought shifts David onto his side;
worry no longer nags at his sleep
now that a solution beckons like a turned down bed.

In the morning emissaries were sent
to Achish, king of Gat, asking for asylum.
Messengers were sent back and forth
until the man from Judah
convinced the Philistine chief

his intentions were honourable,
and received the city of Ziklag in trust.
The camp pulls up stakes
that are never deeply rooted;
everywhere the sound of things coming down:
the whoosh of tents that collapse like dancers,
the clanging of pots brash as whores,
the thud of wool
in the fold upon fold of blankets.
"Aie, ai, ai," the women shriek to God,
their cries a lathe to ease the labour of packing,
while children run rings around their skirts
and dart between the camels,
hoping to salvage a game from another forced march;
but a man's hand lashes out
and his cuff sends them reeling.
Ropes slap on skin and are pulled tight,
the last bundles loaded,
the spears sent fore and aft;
the drivers switch the beasts:
that kneel and rise and trumpet to the sky
their common grief.
Slowly this scrawl of an army sets forth,
a pin-point of fire at its head,
berry-red, the mane proud as a lion's;
behind, a train of camels
drawn like a line through the hills,
hump joined to hump
by the scarlet flecks in rolled up carpets,
or lips clamped for a journey:
the hunted are again on the move,
and like all the hunted,
hope this time they are going home.

David certainly intends it to be.
Ziklag: last stop but one,
and for now last stop, period.
Which is what he would have Achish believe,
and sets about to prove
his ties with Saul are severed forever.

In a little over a year
David and his men amass great wealth:
oxen, sheep, asses galore, fine brocade,
gems that come but yearly in caravans from the East,
and a tenth of what they get they shovel to the king,
the dribblings, David tells him,
of their sallies against Judah
and its borders to the south.
But no such raids ever took place.
Month after month, instead,
the man who smote in the tens of thousands
took his lean guerilla band on forays
against Israel's foes as old as the Exodus;
and putting Samuel's history lessons
to the good use they were intended,
sacked the cities that trailed the names
Geshur, Gezir, Amalek,
torched their fields, stole their harvest, led away their cattle,
after first making sure
the soul of every man, woman and child
was delivered of its body.
No prisoners, he remembered,
and added to God's injunction
the sly reason of survival:
he wanted no Evyatar
crawling to Achish with counter-tales.
And Achish,
in the absence of appropriate witnesses,
wanting to believe, believed what David told him.

Thus, when the Philistines once again
gathered their armies to march against Saul,
the king of Gat had David and his men
enrolled beneath his banner.
But his fellow lords protested:
"What are those Hebrews doing here?
Is that not David whom the women praised while dancing,
saying Saul slew in the thousands
but David in the tens of thousands?
The very one who killed Goliath

and sang his golden harp to the king?"

"Yes," replied Achish, "but Saul's servant is now mine.
Over a year has he sojourned with me
and faultless has he been in all that time.
In Israel itself his name is abhorred
for he has crossed and recrossed the border,
bringing the riches of Judah to Gat;
enough for me to trust him with my head."

"And so lose it. What better way for him
to reconcile himself with Saul
than to offer him your head,
and ours too,
on the end of a javelin?
A man who crosses and recrosses a border
can always go home;
and we can lose the battle before it starts."

They argued back and forth,
but the princes of Palestine were unmoved.
Achish, bowing to numbers, called David to his side:
"My gods know I hold no grudge against you.
Straight have you been with me
since coming to dwell in my land,
and right does it seem that you should be part of my camp.
My fellow lords think otherwise,
and no matter how much I sing your praises
their qualms remain.
Forgive me, my friend, my too little eloquence,
but I must ask you tomorrow to rise with the sun
and return to Ziklag."

Now it was David's chance to protest, and he did:
"But my lord, what have I done?
What harm has your servant caused
that he should be barred from fighting your enemies?
Or is my fault the same and simple one
of being too kind to his king?
I came to you an outlaw,

and I see that an outlaw I remain."

The king, moved to pity, hastens to assure him:
an angel, compares him to an angel,
and wrings his own conscience in regret;
but there are the lords, and begs him not to offend them.
And David, acquiescing,
thinks how all kings are the same;
but his own words have touched him to the quick,
and suddenly he fears
for that king who is his first and only.

3

Saul.
Tower.
Swell of tower.
Rising from the sea twisted and coiled
but still anchored to the depths;
tall curve, bright spume,
glint on the crest of a wave come from afar
to spend itself on the shore.
So many days have passed.
The pain piles up
like dead leaves of old calendars
putting lines in a face,
rounding those noble shoulders.
Still the king rears on his hind legs to piss.
He is alone now. Keeps his own counsel.
Issues decrees.
Stamps and stamps with the royal seal,
his teeth bared and half his mind as well.
More troops.
He wants more troops.
Flint. Iron.
One day marble and silk.
A kingdom, he reminds them,
who are yet content to sleep in sheepfolds.
Samuel dead, he adds
for those who like to forget.
And to make sure there is no backsliding
has his scribe ink on a potsherd:
no necromancy, on pain of exile;

then sends it round to the tribes.
Let them know, he thinks, what it is like
for a king to stand alone before God,
beneath the nation's mantle
a man as naked as anyone,
two bare shoulders, two old tits,
a pair of wrinkled balls
and a knee that aches with the rain;
and above all, worry
as large as an orange in his brain.
The king must rest, Saul announces,
but at night he wanders in his own abode
scratching the walls
and licking the crumbs off stone.
Mornings are worst
when even the damsels are no solace,
and he finally falls asleep
dreaming of harps.
By noon the crown is once again
settled firmly on his head,
and the king does what he has to do
to husband.
Fields and cattle.
Army and wife.
Even supper,
where the open beaks drip blood.
And the sun rises and the sun falls
while David, striking at Amalek,
is forgotten.

But the Philistines have not given up
on turning Saul's life into a chronicle,
and return with their well licked wounds
to the scene of the crime
others call destiny.
Saul lifts up his eyes
again to see smoke on the mountains opposite
rise from the Philistine camp;
and though not surprised, discouraged,
having long been out of the soothsayer business.

The scouts report that their tents stretch to Heaven;
the simple port of arms from place to place
turns the hilltop into a carpet of brass,
and above this molten road
flags from every city down the coast
leap into the blue like uncoiled snakes.

"They have come to try again, Sire, and seriously."

Saul's smile stays trapped in his mouth.
He sees. He hears.
And deep in his being knows
it is more serious than that:
a tremor for a moment slashes his bowels.
He turns to God, and failing God,
he asks his priest for comment,
and when no answer comes
he goes among the prophets,
who can only say the results are inconclusive.
"Jerk the army tight," Saul orders Abner.
"Tomorrow or the day after tomorrow
we'll be going out to battle."

But to himself:
"So many numbers.
I feel I'm facing Heaven's host,
and who of human clay
can fight the angels and win?
Of course it makes no difference.
The Philistines have always wanted my head
and once again I shall give them their chance.
I do not wear the crown for nothing,
and Jonathan must see.
Still, it would be nice to know the odds.
A man ought not to go about blind,
least of all a king to his grave."
And so the king called his servants over,
told them to find him a woman
who conjures up spirits from the dead,
knowing that like all good servants

they must control the contraband;
and sure enough they gave him the name
of a woman from Ein Dor.
Saul changed his clothes, removed his crown,
slung a patch across his eye;
and led by two of his men under cover of night,
paid a visit to their diviner.

A village like any other. A house to match.
The walls square and white, and now imbued with shadow.
His men usher him in, then wait outside like doorposts.
The woman brings fruit and wine on a tray
but Saul waves it away,
thinking how well such kind modesty
decorates a house of ill repute,
and longs momentarily
for such marvellous nondescript.
Anodyne.
And then bestirs himself:
"I need your help to raise a man from the grave."

But the woman answers as is her wont:
"You know the king has forbidden
communion with dead souls,
and threatened those who disturb the spirits
with banishment.
Why then do you come to me
to snare my life in my own living-room?"

The king replies with custom of his own:
"As God is my witness,
I swear no harm shall come to you.
My reach is great and my sway such
that a thousand men will try to knife my eye
before your house is visited by the king.
But since you doubt,
let the silence of the men who guard your door
be surety for my claim."

His argument is strong

and as suasive as his money,
but her sixth sense scratches at the back door of her mind
like a cat in the wee morning hours:
the man's need rises from his armpits.
And yet:
this woman who for so many years
has delved into the mysteries
and felt the heartbreak and terror of men
like sponge moss between her hands,
knows the stink that drives them on
and pities them:
"Whom would you have me raise?"

And the king says:
"Samuel."

The woman tries, but the spirit world resists,
too much bad blood
between the man and the shade;
but Saul's eye continues to beseech her,
a whelp in pain,
and she plays the card of pity
with the ghost.
At length the earth cracks its lid,
and a cloud slides out
from the sarcophagus of human souls.
Looms large; thunder.
Despotic; a voice roaring on a mountain top.
The woman screams to see such fury
nameless, formless, boundless;
mercy injured,
and sparks like a pin-wheel at its heels.
And so cries out,
knowing now it is a case of majesty:
"Why did you trick me? For surely you are Saul."

But Saul, eager as a child at a fire,
brushes back her fear
as though it were a hair that blocked his view:
"Don't be afraid. Only tell me, what do you see?"

And she stammers some nonsense
about God rising from the ground.

"Yes! Yes!" says Saul, "but what does he look like?"

She peers into the darkness and finally sees light:
"An old man. Hoary head.
Ancient bones. Wrapped in a mantle."

Saul knows it must be Samuel and bows twice,
his nose pressed to the ground.
But huddling in his cloak, an iced-over wraith,
Samuel can only ask:
"Why? Why have you hauled me up from the fields of bliss?
I left you my works, did I not? Even my hopes.
But men are such they would rather disturb the dead
than believe their own memories."

Saul hears nothing after the first question.
His whole body is racing;
blood rushes, skin yearns, temples rock,
and the hands grope for the cloak as if it were home;
bed;
sanctuary.
"I'm in a mess. The Philistines are attacking
once again, and God has finally gone.
I've stopped dreaming, and the prophets speak to me
in riddles. There's only you left
to tell me what to do. As once you did,
when first you loved me."

But Samuel is now indifferent to love,
at best remembers how for years
he waited for this moment;
can only repeat the words
which carry a vengeance of their own:
"It is pointless to ask and pointless to tell.
God has done more than leave you,
and is now about to do what He promised

that day you tore my coat and I told you
your kingdom shall be torn and given to another.
Yes, to David; for you would not torch Amalek
with God's anger, and so the fire
you declined to let curry your heart
shall now be turned against you.
Tomorrow you and your sons shall join me,
and the camp of Israel shall be trussed up and delivered
into the hands of the Philistines."

Saul gasps, stumbles,
his son's death rattle in his throat
like the clear bone bauble in his hand
that morning he first entered the nursery;
"No! no!" trapped there in perfect pitch,
unpronounced,
like the long ago joy
come full circle.
Saul hurtles forward,
his full height slams the ground,
the mind refusing to comprehend,
the body unable:
"He is my son, and a son must outlive his father;"
this the last line, the one he will not transgress,
and closes his mouth around it.

The woman is aghast to see the king
lying at her feet.
She rushes to her door to call his men,
her voice hissing panic
like the gruel of excrement
that escapes from the cornered and herded:
"The king! The king has fallen!
And woe is me who will have to explain
why Israel's head rests upon my floor.
Fear not, he said, hinting at great power,
yet what good is a mighty arm
if its owner is asleep, half swooned to death,
and the person he intended to protect
by his very self declared an outcast?

O Lord, God of Israel,
let the king not expire in my house,
or it shall quickly go about
that a woman did him in with her foul spirits;
and they shall come and batter down these walls,
tear my sons from their wives
and mothers from their children,
for it is well known
that the wrath of Benjamin is great and swift
and mean as a cuckold's."

The king's men hasten to reassure her
as they loosen the cloak about his neck,
while throwing a larger and greater one
about his person:
"It's nothing. He's simply weak.
He hasn't touched a morsel of food all day."

For reasons of her own
she joins in this stupid age-old game,
and of these reasons not least
the pain that bolted from his eye,
a soul impaled on bad news
and so forever,
before which nothing will do
save the even older injunction:
"Eat. Do anything but eat."
But like all those
who fall under the heart's penumbra,
Saul refused.
His men insisted,
argued army, country, history.
The woman also brought her wiles to the fray:
"Before I was scared and my lord bid me take courage.
Now my lord is faint, and who can blame him?
The news from the netherworld is black
and wraps his prayers in sackcloth,
but the news is only news about the future.
Meanwhile the king is king; the father, father;
tomorrow a day like any other

the dice are rolled for love and betrayal,
and you shall go forth as you always do
as helpless as the sun.
The only real question is:
do you go sated or hungry?
I have a fatted calf in the house,
let me prepare it for my king;
thus your handmaid begs my lord
to incline himself to reason's voice,
as only a few moments ago
you did command me heed yours.
For what I say surely you must know:
the king shall need his strength, as shall we all."

The men jump in and add their own assent.

"She's right."

"Of course she's right.
Think of ancient Esau
who leapt at his bowl of porridge;
not proud, not proud at all
to savour the earth's delights
and later on let bygones be bygones."

"What say you, then, my lord? Shall we give the day her due?
Rise, shake the darkness from our thoughts,
allow this kind woman to feed her king
and with the king his men?
Or would you crawl upon her floor
back into the womb?"

So two men and a woman kneaded a king's soul,
as soon she kneaded flour
for the unleavened bread she set before them.
And the king ate and his men ate,
until nothing but bones were left.

*

Night crept across the meridian
that divides the hours
between reveille and the dark beatitudes,
and as it did Saul crawled into bed and slept;
soundly, deeply,
his mind white and scorched
like the ground before Abraham
after God had passed between the pieces.
Then a starfish climbed over the edge of the world
and it was morning.
Gold.
The sky, the air,
the dew that purled the hilltops into earrings
from which the dross of war would soon pour forth:
men turned into enemies by virtue of a name,
an idol,
a camp that eyeballed another.
And so it was.
Men stirred from their dreams.
The rich buckled brass.
The almost rich girded their swords.
The king's minions bent to their bows.
Behind, between, the ranks of thousands
clutching the age-old tools:
spear, axe, scythe if need be,
even the club or sling
that would rip off a head.
And before them kings and princes
prancing like effigies on coins.
So too Saul,
who rides the day's task
instead of a future;
stands before his army like Heaven's tent-pole
and calls his men to order:
"Soldiers of Israel!
Again you are assembled;
again asked to defend lines drawn across the earth.
Some may be tired, I can well understand.
Some must wonder how it is
we have not yet dealt the Philistines a death blow,

and some of you must wonder if ever we shall.
There may even be those weary enough
to think that if they want our land so badly
a way can be found to sue for peace everlasting.
That too I can well understand.
Who does not long for the simple life?
To rise in the morning to his fields and beasts
and return with the evening to his home?
To sit under a tamarisk tree
and reach for the figs on a plate
while the children run after a goat
and a skirt rustles in the dimness?
That is the promise, is it not,
has been ever since we stormed out of Egypt,
but you know as well as I
how blood flows before milk and honey.
A promise forever weeps,
and men are moved to pity their love,
but pity is as useless as a dream
when love at sword-point is forced to beg.
Nothing, therefore, can concern you more
than those few paltry lines we call a border,
nothing more draw your ire
than this latest assault of the Philistines
who would wear you down with their attacks
as recurrent as the rainfall.
For twenty years have I fought them,
and if anyone should be tired
it is surely I;
but each time they invade my blood is roiled
that they dare still covet our women and children,
cattle and harvests, cities and altars,
and above all else begrudge us our God
rather than settle for peace.
Know then that it shall never stop,
our God is but the pretext for all the rest,
and the Philistines His instrument
to beat us into an army.
Listen, my people, to your king
who like you was once content

to follow the trail of stray donkeys:
even the path that leads to the furrows of barley
ends in a war.
Turn then your minds from the sorrows of deliverance
and wake to the task at hand;
on yonder hill the enemy stirs
who would rake your country with fire
and turn a life-long battle
into a conflagration.
This you cannot allow,
for unto no man is it given to abdicate,
least of all a subject
who demanded of a prophet a king;
and what is a king without his sovereign land?
Courage, then, I say;
be alert, yield not,
let God again take care of His people."

Thus did Saul find the words
to rouse a war cry from his regiments' throats,
and as it flew into the air
the two camps flew into the valley,
a screech of birds in armour:
swords flail and hack at leather-strapped limbs,
spears hiss into soft flesh,
arrows pierce eyes, throats, a half-turned temple,
and bodies fall halved and quartered,
blood spurting into the azured canopy
endless as wine at an endless wedding,
and the firmament rent with agony
ripped from the chests of men
whose lives fly up like feathers
at a fire in an aviary
Saul sees it is raining death.
To his right, where once a wall of men
had studded the hill half-way round its waist,
lay the trampled brains of those
who had only their fists left
to take on the Philistine hooves.
Their flank unguarded, the king's troops could only parry

and pray for a miracle,
but the enemy allowed no time for prayer,
pressed the Israelites like wood chips
against the slopes of Gilboa
and then sent in their reserves,
who caught the valiant and the wayward and drove them back
until shafts sliced through liver and groin
and nailed them to the ground.
Retreat, then, though not yet a rout:
the cry of the sword still confused
with the cry of the slain,
and Saul climbs the hill backwards,
cleaved from his main body of troops
now mauled to pockets.
And so they fight: fathers, sons, captains of hosts
and the faithful they still inspire,
for above all there is honour;
a word spoken by a king.
But the king, head and shoulders above any man,
sees what they cannot,
sees how each minute each band of men
is whittled by Philistine iron
until when next he looks he cannot see his sons,
not Avinadav, not Malkishua,
and even his cherished, scolded Jonathan
he only glimpses as the haft of a heathen spear
sails through his neck.
Saul's own jerks back and his heart explodes
in pain, in grief, in splattered rage
at the mighty fist of God descending on his house;
but the howl that split him from skull to toe
leaps to his mouth and dies there:
between that instant Saul's world foreclosed
and the flash of his humbled fury,
a Philistine let loose an arrow that struck the king;
then another, and another,
and the king reels like a sick porcupine.
Saul's armour-bearer rushes to his side,
but his arm is too weak to raise a sword.
Dust of death in his nostrils. Carrion-sore eyes.

Israelites falling everywhere,
their ranks thinner than lean meat at the butcher's,
so thin the enemy could wheel
its seven princes through in triumph.

"Damn," cries Saul,
his life turning on its axis of woe,
ready to fold;
and to the lad who brought him weapons to battle on:
"Hurry! Draw your sword and thrust me through
before those foreskinned soldiers lay their hands
on this royal dying body.
We have been at ruthless war so long
I fear what may befall."
But when he sees the lad shrink
from skewering the man who wears the crown,
he aims straight for those startled eyes:
"Think how they will sneer
as they strip my body of its raiment
and hold up the manhood of Israel's throne
to jibe and ridicule,
while I hang with life
limp enough to see my shame
but too weak to end it."
Yet those eyes still say no,
and Saul sees the shame they fear
when later on ten thousand pairs will ask
how a man who bore arms to shield a king
could turn them on his master;
and so, to spare this youth
no closer to the king
than any of the vagrants
recommended to his service,
Saul turns his own blade toward his belly
and falls on it.

Poor youth! so young, so burning bright,
so ardent in his reverence
for all that smacks of power's majesty,
he does not see the king tossed him his life

like coins dropped into a busker's suitcase;
sees only honour kept to the very end,
that sweeps him up into its tormented brilliance
and flush onto his sword.
Thus did they all die: Saul, and Saul's three sons,
his armour-bearer and thousands of his men,
the number of the slain only counted
by the wails that shrieked their twisted way to heaven
from every house to which no man returned;
and the cities, now barren of their soldiers,
were abandoned to the enemy.

But before the Philistines moved in
they scoured the hillside for royal remains,
and coming upon Saul and his three sons
severed their lifeless torsos from their heads;
then quietly, expertly,
stripped each carcass of its armour,
heaved the pierced and rotting flesh into a wagon,
but the lustrous swords and jewelled scabbards
and oxhide shields rimmed with beaten silver
and leaf-thin brass body suits with helmet
they parcelled out with care among the chariots
and then drove off,
leaving to the vultures that circle in the mute sky
what once meant all but now in death is worthless:
two eyes, a pair of ears,
the ever mysterious lips.
and that in royal outline four times over.
Home, the Philistines took their shining plunder
and hung it in those houses
where gods and men meet in worship,
but the bodies of Saul and his three sons
they nailed to the walls of Beit Shean,
confident that a king's corpse
dangling from those ramparts
would do as well as any runners;
and so the story of Saul's disgrace
passed quickly down the caravan trails
to pollinate men's hearts.

But when it reached the precincts of Yavesh-gilead
at once the men slapped on their armour
and force-marched through the night,
as stone-faced as the moon and just as swift,
their armour nothing more than bitter memory.
It was still the time of judges;
their elders had refused
to join the rest of Israel
in war against their brother Benjamin
for crimes so heinous they demanded blood,
and paid for their refusal by going up in smoke,
all but four hundred virgins
rescued from the slaughter
to serve as wives to outlawed Benjamin,
when once the rest of Israel did repent
of their harsh and rash decree
forbidding intermarriage with the sinners.
And so in the time of kings
the offspring of this patched-up union
found themselves one daybreak
staring at the shadows of Saul and his three sons
spread-eagled on a city's walls.
Staring but a moment:
they quickly cut the corpses down,
pulled the putrid entrails from their sun-burned skins,
washed and cleaned the rest, then laid them out in scarlet silks
and bore them thus on litters to Yavesh,
where in silence grim and dispatch royal
they burned their first king's last remains
down to the bone.
And when the fire had consumed all that it could eat,
they gathered up those bones over which they wept
and buried them.
Thus Saul found the rest he craved
under a tamarisk tree,
and the men of Yavesh fasted seven days.

But no one, least of all a king,
slips away as if he's never been,

as though he were a wind that uprooted nothing,
carried no spores, found no cheek
to graze with a message of love.
And so when one man dies many must mourn.

*

Blue.
So blue the sky.
As if some royal engineers' battalions
had scraped and sanded every pane
to cerulean perfection.
And in that blue so flawless
that his heart knelt at its own rage,
smoke.
Cruel.
Twisting its way into that God-blown dome
and running the cobalt blue to arsenic white.

A mishap, David thinks,
like people frying beans in a temple.
But nearing Ziklag he fears disaster,
and spurs his horse and men toward the town.
Disaster it is.
Half-burned houses half standing.
Dogs that limp their way through fallen rafters,
their seared flesh chased by flies.
And everywhere silence.
No arm howls for its shoulder.
No maiden sobs for charms
assaulted by a foreign penis.
Only the ash-white quiet
after fire has scoured a city
and licked it clean as a plate;
a still desert wind fanning embers,
and smoke, like an iron, curling the sky.
But somewhere in these blasted ruins
two crones and their husband sit against a wall,
eyes forever fixed on the camels
that crashed through their lives

and the riders that scooped up their daughters,
daughters' daughters and sons too,
and left them to burn like straw.
"Eye for eye and tooth for tooth,"
they dribbled through the holes between their teeth,
and David knew it was Amalek.
Old war. Old enemy.
A snake biting at his heel
and he dumb enough to forget,
thinking himself so clever
because the king of Gat was a fool,
and now stands a ruined gambler between two wars,
his hands clutching at the head
they would bang against a wall.
And so he does what any man would do
when luck has whistled down his dreams of glory
and looped them like a wire across his path.
He cries.
As do his men,
each for the wife no longer wife
who sweeps the doorstep with reproach
and sifts him like flour
through the different degrees of beholden,
down to the breakfast lineup
of the ragamuffins he has sired
until caught, a nail on a thread,
in her burnoused love;
but for her who came to him once mantled in flowers
and anointed his lips with her breasts,
and for those abducted with her,
the little ones who came into the light
from such sweet and sweated straining.
And so unbounded grief
caterwauls to the stony hills,
and their cries rise and rise
as if God Himself had rummaged in their diaphragms
until they can no more.
Slowly their chests subside
to the normal bob of a buoy in water,
and David's men take stock:

exile abroad and exile at home,
cold in their spines, fire on their cheeks,
trackers always at their heels,
the years like their camp move in a blur
toward a promise,
and the promise as faithful as the inverse square
of the distance from moon to man;
their city evaporated,
their children turned to angel paste,
and in the dust that filters everything but pain
above the rock and stubborn root,
they hear them captive, moan.

Rage, then;
and then despair,
like soft rain after hard.
The length of their days in bitter writ
unscrolls before their eyes,
and they reach for words as if they were stories
to hurl against their chief
and grind their misery into his bones.
David hears the murmur of rebellion
and runs for the ephod,
snaps his fugitive priest to life
and has him hold the holy vestment up.
"Higher," he orders.
"Now tilt it down,"
hoping like Moses,
when he waved those tables of the Law
before his calf-besotted children,
to scare his men out of their sorrow-crazed wits.
The jewelled eye of God dazzles,
the grumbling crowd shuffles to a halt;
in the lull between despair and disbelief
David enters,
soft as a dancer steals upon her beloved,
and breaks their ears with his address:
"My men, my prized and faithful men
whom loyalty has already made to suffer much.
Do not for a minute think I hurt

any less than you.
For years the man I love the most
has been kept beyond my reach;
and I,
to save a priest, a people,
a kingdom if not the king himself,
kept beyond his.
For my efforts I was mocked;
when not mocked, hounded;
when not caught, reviled.
Who in this land has not chuckled
to tell how David fled from the king's spear
by sliding down his wife's bedsheets?
Who not think him weak and foolish
to twice return that self-same king his spear
and in exchange watch helpless from afar
as the monarch transferred his daughter
from Bethlehem to Gallim?
Twice and twice that over
have I lost my love and love's companion,
and now again I stand a humble witness
to loss much multiplied by yours.
Already I hear the wicked tongues let loose:
'The man who would be king has overreached himself.
He thought his name a garrison enough
and so left Ziklag undermanned.
He thought his foreign liege-lord in his pocket,
only to find that bribes and stories
were no match for the arsenal of princes
when they leaned on a king weak enough to take them,
and so had to leave Israel fend for herself.'
For once the wicked tongues are right.
I erred; and many for my error will pay.
But why compound the fault with scorn?
Is it not enough that the dogs will yap
in the lands of Judah's neighbours,
the bulls of Bashan laugh themselves silly?
Or must you sweeten our enemies' glee
by despising our own shame?
Nothing I assure you would please them more

than one day to have it told
how David's men rose like lions
and tore his flesh from his bones;
then wiped their hands across their mouths
and curled their lips at courage."

Pauses here, and sniffs the air
to check if the wind blows courage or shame,
but the men's bodies are undecided.
At least that, he thinks, and pushes on:
"If that is what you want I give you that.
And yet I am loathe
to offer you my limbs for supper.
For years have we rode together,
eaten the same food, swallowed the same dust,
borne insults from the same fools.
There were times when the only food was dust,
the only greeting insult,
times when all we did was flee
and others when it looked as though
our next breath were our last.
And yet you did not desert.
Alone in my tent I cried to God:
how much and how long must a man endure?
And when the answer out of His silence came back:
as much and as long as the grass must bear
the men and women who tread upon it,
I bent my tentflap back to watch
the little movements of our lives
and saw you go about your faith
in a thousand gestures of war and peace
that now you would abandon.
And who can blame you?
Why, you may well ask, should a sentry now stand watch?
What boy is there to pound the grain?
What woman to scan for afternoon spies
before she follows her arm into her shelter?
I too have had my faith
sliced at the kneecaps.
I look on our heap of desolate ash

and think how my clattered bones would stare
at their lonely severed legs,
and my heart sinks lower than the slave-pit
where once Joseph lay in darkness,
and whines for the jackals to come and feast.
And yet, though my bowels melt
and my tongue cleaves to its palate,
I will not yield
until God Himself heaves me into the ground.
For He Who lowers also raises;
He Who sends enemies also sends help;
and until both my wives lie in my two arms,
the earth shall not breathe free of my horses' hooves.
If you ride with me,
into the Lord's praise."

And the priest waved the ephod and shouted:
"Ride. For you shall overtake them.
And save your own, as surely as you once saved me."

And six hundred men bellowed back their assent:
"Ride."

And:
"Ride."

And again:
"Ride."

And overhead, the blue sky cracked its aching canvas.

*

Men build cities
where fault lines run the earth,
and from dreams where exiled serpents talk
harangue the noonday crowds.
So courage rides on the debris of despair.
So David's men
over the pebbles of their angry hearts.

Through the blameless air they fly,
indifferent to the gnats their flight surprises,
their eyes fixed on the stingy ground
for the snagged bush and disturbed stone
and the unintended prints of herd and flock
that passed in wanton number,
and in their ears the terrible whisper:
"Hurry! Hurry!"
whipping their hearts that now start to squirm
at the thought their delay in Ziklag
will prove fatal as well as stupid;
and so press on, relentless,
against the relentless land,
a dropped horizon of brown and grey
shrunk to perfection like blown glass
that sucks the breath from their lungs
and leaves them worn and weary
when they reach the brook at Besor:
six hundred men at the water's edge
like a daisy chain of wilted alveoli,
and of the six two hundred are so faint
they go no further;
yet before the rest depart,
fish from the grasses that guard the brook
a half-dead soul whose eyes in terror speak
a fate as hapless as their own.
A host of hands appear. Some prop him up,
others bring bread and water to his lips.
"Not enough," a knowing voice calls out
like some warden for the almost gone,
and other long-stemmed fingers quickly crumble
half a fig-cake into the stranger's mouth,
then press raisin after raisin
onto his awakened tongue
until that same all-knowing voice,
or perhaps his brother's,
orders them to stop:
"Enough. Now someone go fetch David."

Who comes.
Fast and bearing down,
red and gold ablaze
like fire of garnet and amber,
staring down the famished man's eyes
with a hunger all his own.
Who asks:
"Whose are you?"
for the ear is pierced and the tunic bare.
And:
"Where do you come from?"

"From Egypt," the young man says, wishing it were so,
"but I am servant to an Amalekite,
who left me here when I fell sick
three days ago."

David winces.
Three days.
Time enough to unravel light and darkness,
and watch the spear-tip thrust and slice
the belly of all creation.

The slave, now half alive and half unbent
like a jack-knife at right angles to its clasp,
sees the tiny vessels in David's eyes
burst with might-have-been-shed blood,
and in his own the wide blue fingered delta
that flows over and through the fields
like a woman over and through her lover,
waves lapping the mind they bear
to might-have-been home and yet-to-be life
if only he too can promise
hope's soft caress.
"When the news arrived that the Philistines
had gone to war against Israel,
my Amalek lords supposed
their garrisons somewhat depleted
and so struck, deep into the land of the Cherethites,
for they were nearest and sweetest

and their cities beckoned like a fat thigh to a dog,
but since one bite will never suffice, they pushed south
to the border outposts of Caleb and Judah
where we skimmed the sparse land
of its even sparser inhabitants
before reaching Ziklag which we put to the torch.
Then, their ardour cooled and the camp weighed down
with the immense booty of human slaves
and foot-dragging cattle and dumb directionless sheep,
the troop set their faces north."

Slaves, cattle, sheep;
the arithmetic of life,
and David's heart leapt
the way rams crack a hilltop
or the Jordan rolls its current:
his wives are alive,
his wives and all their wives,
trudging in a convoy's dust
north to freedom;
and like a man who steps outside his house
to see his future, he asks this servant
forced to change his master:
"North is a point. Many highways lead there.
Will you who know the road their feet must take
conduct me to this troop?"

And this man unused to conducting anyone
now trades his promise for another:
"Swear to me by your God
that you will neither kill me
nor hand me over to my master,
and I shall lead you to them."

David swears.

The man leads.

In two days they have caught up with their quarry,
a column the length of a valley

that moves as one but is not one:
in the center the women and children
weary and stumbling,
at their side the small-horned beasts that follow the ground,
their hides from a distance linked and flapping
like a rug in the wind,
and on their flanks cameled Amalek
prod and laugh and swell their chests
to the applause of rocks.
Then evening comes and the trek halts
and the men dismount and turn the camp
into a dancing wheel;
and the jug is passed and the animals slaughtered,
and the jug again passed and with it the meat,
and once more the jug like a sentry makes the rounds,
and the men sink their arms into their plunder,
and the wind carries their delight
until high in the thinning air it crumbles
and falls at David's feet.
Who stares,
as stares a man who looks in disbelief
upon his own footprints;
draws back his hand to fling it forward
and so sicks Judah's fury on their rivals.
Four hundred foaming men
race the dust from lookout to plain
and hack away at the spectacle
of an open-air brothel:
the nude buttocks that greet their swords,
the pendant testicles lopped so cleanly
they could be served for dinner;
half-naked men running for cover
with blood spurting from their eyes or throats.
But there is no cover, only escape,
and the camels are finite in number.
So Amalek does what enemies always do:
regroups, stands, fights,
hoping to vanquish by weight and endurance.
But David's men are too enraged
to be impressed by odds;

and thus from twilight to twilight
litter this land of stone with corpses.

When evening comes again
David stares out at a new ruin.
Pride no longer galls his tongue like coriander.
The body count is all in their favour:
four hundred Amalekite youths fled on camels,
the rest turned to fertilizer;
on their side only minor casualties:
each man has back his wife, sons, daughters,
while David, in addition to his wives,
can reckon with the spoils.
He does, his mind already toting up
the assets they represent:
friends he can keep, others he can acquire,
above all a good name to peddle at the court;
perhaps, just perhaps,
the king at last can be made to see
his son's lover is no more a threat
than a spider on a palace wall,
and so exchange his iron grip for a lighter touch.
"Ziklag was burned," he longs to tell Saul,
"the city I got from the Philistine king
and roofed with gold
from sallies against our enemies.
Yes, ours; for Achish only saw
the semblance of our vendetta.
How could he know I moved away
to protect your royal person,
just as you could hardly know
that for much the same reason Jonathan moved closer?
All was fine until I forgot
that craft could outsmart itself.
There are those who never stopped playing
by the hard and fast rule of old:
you are for me or against me
for ever and ever.
And they did me in,
kept me from the Philistine ranks

where I might have done Israel some good,
while their low and wretched neighbours
sacked my city.
Burned everything.
Carried off all that could be carried off.
We pursued them.
Overtook them.
Overcame.
Got all back and more.
But we almost did not pursue,
almost were overcome
by the hatred within the cone of burning black.
It was then, Sire, I swore
if God Whose fire consumes all fires
comes once again to my rescue,
I shall crawl with my victory to your court
and beg for reprieve;
for I am tired, my lord, of running
from a man I have no wish to run from,
and from his son for whom I burn
as others burned for my city."
So David tells himself,
dazzled by the power of his plunder.

But when he and his plunder reach Besor
the troops who followed him into combat
object to the division of spoils:
"To those too weak to fight
let their wives and children be returned
but nothing more,
for booty is the prize of those who risk."

Another old rule, thinks David,
and counters with the hard silk tones of mercy:
"No, my brothers,
for though, as you say, we took the risk,
the victory is not ours to claim.
By any common measure of war
the slaughter should have gone the other way.
With four times the number of troops

and hostages so dear they tied our hearts,
Amalek had us licked
before they even began to pray;
only they reckoned not
with the God That fights at our side,
Who pumps courage beyond reason into our veins
but draws our enemies into sloth
with the poverty of our numbers.
There is your risk:
vigilance grown slack,
a camp turned into a carnival.
And how far a cry from our own deceit
when first faced with the rubble of Ziklag
we turned inward to despair and reproach
and sought, like the first of men's brothers, for stones?
What restrained us but the voice
that knows we are only woven figures
in the seamless shawl of time,
who grow now faint, now stout of heart,
the one no less than the other
the consequence for men when God takes a nap?
What justice then for your claim
that would deny our spoils
to those who were merely faint of limb?
None, my brothers, I say again;
instead, let it henceforth be inscribed
in the annals of our law
that all have their share in the trophies of war,
as much they who tarry by the baggage
as those who go down to battle."

And so it was, and more:
each man given his allotment,
but the lion's part set aside
for David to pursue his plans.
And so when all and sundry of their troop
had reentered what was left of Ziklag,
David sent round gifts to the elders of Judah,
each ox and bracelet
announcing his thanks to God Almighty,

while elsewhere he turned the booty into tribute
to weld an alliance:
Beit-El and Ramat-Negev, Yattir and Anoer,
Siphmot, Eshtemoa, and Rachal
where honey is cut from rock,
the cities of the Yerachmeelites
and the cities of the Kaynites,
also to Horma, Chor-ashan, Attach,
and unto Hebron where Abraham spread his tents
under the terebinths of Mamre.

*

Bricks. Stone. Mortar.
All in place and then one day dislodged,
by act of man or God it's all the same;
brings you face to face with dust and soot
and the broken blocks of men's
craving for the heavens.

So Ziklag sits in the eyelash of its hills and smoulders;
burnt brick, burnt stone, all its props askew.
Thousands of hands sift through the cinders
to see what can be salvaged.
For three days they have been at work
sorting, cleaning, stacking:
the whole and the broken,
the still good and the hopelessly ruined,
like the blessings and curses
of Aval and Gerizim.
The smell of fire is everywhere
like the sick smell of lilies in a room,
but out of that they fashion beginnings:
ovens, tables, an altar;
sometimes do no more than requisition
what the fire has scooped out
Thus it is that when a man with rent clothes
and ashes on his head
drags himself through Ziklag's embers
to prostrate himself at David's feet,

he finds upon looking up
he is looking at a monument:
the red hair burned to orange by the sun
falls in streaks like thinly braided tears
onto a leather tunic,
once brown, now caramel,
cracked by desert grief to form a coat of mail
one with the staggered brick
on which he sits as on a throne,
makeshift and colossal,
as though the Sphinx had finally crawled north
in an exodus all his own.
But the lips move:
"Why this garb? And why here?
Can't you see we've had our fill of missing persons,
or do you think by bringing sackcloth
to a house of mourning,
like a cup of honey to the neighbours,
we will extend an invitation
to misery and her mercy?"

No answer to this broadside.
The man, like David's own, has lost his tongue
until Avishai steps forward with his spear
and prods him into speech.
"I come from Israel's camp," he says.
"The people are fallen or fled;
the king and his sons dead."

Words that cut creation at the jugular;
stop all further speech,
or turn the flow to blood.
Avishai's spear falls to the ground and clatters.
Iron on stone.
The sound of love lost to a wretched heart.
Only that,
and the embarrassment of men,
who look to the statue of red brick
and wait for it again to speak.
Now sepulture and throne, it does;

and David, like all those dazed before and since,
asks for proof.
Details.
The ones needed for the death certificate.
And so his voice, dry and lifeless,
though from this side of the tomb,
puts the question:
"How do you know that Saul and his sons are dead?"

And the man who lugged his show of grief to Ziklag,
answers:
"By chance I was on mount Gilboa,
and at that spot where Saul was leaning on his spear,
the life half dribbled out of him,
but only half; the rest turned toward the thunder
of fast pressing horse and chariot.
Yet out of the corner of his eye he spied me
and called me over.
I went.
'Who are you?' he asked.
'An Amalekite,' I said.
'Then pray, stand over me and slay me,' he said,
'for though I die, I yet have life,
only not enough to end it.'
And certain that his words were true —
for no man could recover from his blows —
I stood at his side and slew him."
But knowing that his story
could easily be dismissed as hearsay,
the man reaches into his cloak
for the exhibits to prove his claim,
and hands to the man he calls 'my lord'
the crown he took from the king's head
and the bracelet he took from his arm:
"So my lord will know I also speak the truth."
And bows again.

David takes these marks of royal presence
and fingers every ridge and jewel
as if they would recount the years:

Saul chagrined in his tent
thrusting his armour upon him,
Jonathan by the rock slipping him his body,
the court days sliding between harp and spear,
the maidens' praise and the king's brooding,
Michal coiled about his sex
until rage got the better of them all,
turned cruel,
and split a perfect world in two and three
and now in many pieces,
the last of which are these.
And putting down the crown
that others would have placed upon his head,
he tears his clothes, rip by careful rip,
then reaches down to their ashen earth
for the handfuls of dirt he rubs into his hair
and sits there, more motionless than ever,
until evening.
His men, in fealty and trial sworn, do likewise,
and likewise do their women;
and so to the odour of fire is added
the wail of lamentation.
But in those moments he could cry no more
and his broken heart could break in no more pieces,
David thought:
"Again, Amalek!
Are we never to be rid of this curse?
The same that would rape my wife
has killed my king,
and no doubt would have killed my lover
had it suited his design.
He says the king was weak and certain to expire.
But how weak? And how close to his death?
And why bring me the crown with his story?
Perhaps the crown was stolen
and headed for another souk
when the man got word we trounced his fellow thieves
and changed his plans,
decided to fence both crown and story,
bribing thus the new king

with the murder of the old.
But who said I was king apart from Samuel dead?
Just think how it will play when the news gets about
that David was anointed sovereign
by an Amalekite:
a put up job, they will murmur,
and turn me from an outlaw into a traitor,
and thence to usurper.
Once again this nation that has always bit our heels
will clip us from behind,
sow dissension in an already fertile field,
and the four hundred youths who fled on their camels
will nurse the sting of their defeat with laughter
at the way we burn each other's houses.
No. A thousand times no.
Samuel would never have approved;
nor Jonathan, who was content to be my prince
yet stuck by his father.
O my love, to think you dead –
for surely you would not alive have let
these royal baubles come into my possession –
to think you dead I want to take this stranger
and shake him until all the world's shame
is fallen from his bones
for having dared think I would be glad
to see this crown that always came between us
lie so at my feet."
But then the other words would start again
like a chain of sorrow in his head:
"O my love. O my love."
And then:
"It is more than I can bear;"
those poor half-true lines
because we have no other.
And so David swung between sob and doubt,
until the setting of the sun
nearly nailed his eyes to his silence
and broke it on the cusp of his anger,
the question leaping from his mouth
like a panther to its prey:

"How did your hand not tremble
to slaughter the Lord's anointed?"

And the young stranger so stunned
he said nothing.
But David wants an answer;
wants to hear the young man say:
'It was not I. It did not happen.
The crown at your feet is only
a calling card from your lover.'
Instead silence. Pursed lips.
Aghast so widely shared
you could hear the evening breeze
flutter over ashes.
And the young man stands there glued to his amazement.
Not David,
who strikes with his tongue
as his uncle would raise a cudgel
to the village idiot:
"O rotten man, and a stranger too,
who bears these tales of malice to our camp
and then, perverse like all his people,
shuts his mouth.
But I will have an answer to my question;"
and his lips engorged with the blood they thirst for
fire like a catapult:
"Avishai, strike him,
that I may hear him speak."

Cultured for years
like a pearl in an exquisite oyster,
Avishai strikes;
but his blow, like his master's voice,
is a little bit too hard,
and the Amalekite slumps forever to the ground.
Lungs snap to,
breaths are caught like coats in a door,
and Avishai, dumbstruck at what his hand has done,
can only stammer tears.
David wipes them dry:

"The man's own tongue condemned him,
announcing how he slew the Lord's anointed
without a hint of shame;"
not adding that now the blood is spilled
his own grows quiet;
nor that the world is ever thus from end to end,
not one story but two
going back to the beginning:
there was nothing and there was something,
a man was made from a word
and fashioned from mist,
a snake spoke to a woman
and the woman spoke to man,
there was a quarrel in some field
about some sacrifice.
And thinking of his own,
which coiled around his now dead love
like a circle round a stick
and yet looked to the future
because the future stretches flat before the living,
David lifts the saddest voice his men have ever heard
to praise the fallen:
"Weep, O Israel, for your heroes
slain on the heights of Gilboa.
Weep, daughters of Jacob,
for the man who draped you in scarlet
and wrapped your wrists in gold,
lest it be told in Gat,
or trumpeted in the streets of Ashkelon,
that Saul was king to a thankless people
and his reign, the feeble foolish error
of the circumcised.
For let it not be forgotten:
Saul set out to search for stray donkeys
and found you, a nation of strays,
patchwork of quarrels,
sniping at your judge and whining for a king
to catch up with your neighbours.
And from your neighbours he did defend you
time and time again,

his valiant arm never tired
to plunge its sword deep into the enemy's thigh
until, at last, their fat proved too much
and his shield slipped from his grasp and ours
to lie like lonely iron in a field.
O cursed be that field;
may it know neither rain nor dew
and the mountain slope grow bald with sorrow:
for a king has died there, the Lord's anointed,
and with the king his son whose faithful bow
could not alone have shot across the sky
a hail of arrows so thick it would have silenced
the twang and thwack of the Philistine archers.
Therefore, ye sons of Judah,
take up the bow and learn your craft;
it is enough that I have lost
the man I hold most dear upon this earth.
O my brother,
who would not leave his father to the wolves of his mind,
although that very father
had hurled his javelin into the wall
and let it hang there, token wedge
between his son's body and his son's soul;
and of that soul I so much a part
I grieve and grieve and can do naught but grieve
for such beauty slaughtered on the summits:
I shall miss you,
miss the stubble of your beard that scratched against my cheek,
the cup of your hands, the flow of your loins,
miss the bitter words in the bitter laugh
that wanted the world so perfect,
and so shall long for all that might have been
in all good time,
as you did once foretell
and then bid me be patient.
Of what use now patience?
Of what use anything but regret
and even then?
My love, my love,
let the wind carry these words to the ears of the dead,

and if the dead hear not,
at least the living and the living to come shall know:
great was your love and to me most wondrous,
passing the love of women.
Weep, weep, O Israel,
for Saul and for Jonathan,
beloved and lovely in their lives
now gone to their deaths;
they were swifter than eagles,
they were stronger than lions,
but now gone to their deaths.
How are the mighty fallen,
and the weapons of war perished!"